Grabbing America by the P

Grabbing America by the P

The Redefinition of Power, Truth, and Consequence

Montez DeCarlo

Copyright © 2026 Montez DeCarlo

All rights reserved. No part of this book may be reproduced or transmitted in any form or by any means without the written permission of the publisher, except for brief quotations in reviews.

This book is a work of nonfiction. Interpretations and opinions expressed herein are those of the author and are based on public statements, official actions, and documented events.

ISBN: 979-8-218-90738-9
Imprint: Turtle Island Imprints
Printed in the United States of America

This book relies exclusively on public statements, official actions, court rulings, and documented outcomes. Interpretations reflect the author's analysis and opinion, offered in the interest of historical record and public accountability. Welcome to the author's Podcast in Print.

Contents

PROLOGUE: THE SHARPIE MOMENT 7

PART I— PRACTICE ROUND 1

CHAPTER 1: CROWD CONTROL 1

CHAPTER 2: NATO? NEVER HEARD OF HER 4

CHAPTER 3: GEOGRAPHY IS FAKE NEWS 7

CHAPTER 4: DIPLOMACY, BUT LOUDER 10

CHAPTER 5: FINLAND HAS A BROOM 15

CHAPTER 6: EVERYONE'S A WITCH 19

CHAPTER 7: SHARPIEGATE 24

CHAPTER 8: PANDEMIC CONFIDENCE 29

CHAPTER 9: BALLOTS GONE WILD 34

CHAPTER 10: WHEN WORDS WALK 39

PART II— INTERMISSION 44

CHAPTER 11: STREAMING DEMOCRACY 44

CHAPTER 12: CAMPAIGNING FROM COURTROOMS 48

PART III — THE SEQUEL 52

CHAPTER 13: BACK LIKE A RERUN 52

CHAPTER 14: ACCELERATION WITHOUT CONSTRAINT 55

CHAPTER 15: LOYALTY AS QUALIFICATION 59

CHAPTER 16: GOVERNING BY PERMANENT CRISIS 65

CHAPTER 17: FOREIGN POLICY BY VIBE 69

CHAPTER 18: LAW AND ORDER AS SPECTACLE 76

PART IV 80

CHAPTER 19: THE LAW BENDS SOUTH 80

CHAPTER 20: ARSONIST AS FIREFIGHTER 85

CHAPTER 21: PEACE, LOUDLY... 88

CHAPTER 22: CLEAN HANDS, FULL POCKETS 92

CHAPTER 23: CARVING THE NAME INTO HISTORY 98

CHAPTER 24: JUSTICE, AIMED.. 104

CHAPTER 25: THE FRIEND YOU NEVER KNEW 110

POSTSCRIPT: THIS IS NOT THE END 116

PROLOGUE: THE SHARPIE MOMENT

It begins, as so many things in this era do, with a picture.

Not a policy document. Not a law. Not a dense briefing memo or a carefully drafted executive order that will take months to interpret and years to unwind. A photograph. Laminated. Official. A government-issued weather map designed to communicate certainty in a moment when uncertainty was the norm.

Someone has drawn on it.

The line is thick, dark, and unmistakable. It curves outward into a state the storm never threatens, extending the boundary of danger just enough to rescue a statement already made. The alteration is crude, not because it lacks skill, but because it lacks hesitation. It is drawn with confidence, as if daring the room to object—not to the inaccuracy, but to the authority behind it.

This was not a mistake.

Mistakes retreat when corrected. They soften. They apologize. They accept revision. They dissolve under evidence.

This did not.

Experts have already spoken. Meteorologists clarified publicly and repeatedly. Agencies tasked with public safety issued formal statements explaining the actual forecast. The system did what it was designed to do: identify an error, correct it, and move forward.

The correction was rejected.

That rejection was the moment.

Because what was being challenged was not a forecast. It was the hierarchy. Evidence was no longer the arbiter. Authority was. And authority, once asserted publicly, cannot be seen retreating without consequence. The line remained. The map stayed altered. The room was expected to accept it.

Reality bends—not because it must, but because it is being told to.

The Sharpie itself was trivial. No policy hinged on the altered line. No law changed because of it. No immediate harm resulted from the drawing. And that was precisely why it mattered. This was a low-stakes confrontation with reality, chosen because it was safe to lose.

If reality could be publicly edited here without consequence, it could be edited anywhere.

This moment established a governing instinct that would repeat itself again and again: when faced with contradiction, do not adjust—assert. When faced with expertise, do not engage—dominate. When faced with errors, do not correct—outlast.

The Sharpie moment is not about the weather.

It is about posture.

It revealed how authority was now performed. Correction was reframed as insubordination. Expertise was recast as hostility. Institutions were pressured not to clarify, but to accommodate. Truth became something to defend rather than something to discover.

The public response followed a familiar arc. Laughter arrived first. Memes bloomed instantly. Late-night monologues sharpened their knives. The absurdity felt comforting. It signaled that the moment was too ridiculous to be dangerous.

But comedy was not the correction.

It was anesthetic.

The laughter absorbed the shock without resolving the underlying problem. The moment passed without consequence. No apology arrived. No acknowledgment followed. The alteration remained unaddressed, and then it disappeared from the news cycle entirely.

The system learned something.

It learned that reality could be challenged publicly and survive the challenge. It learned that outrage burns quickly. It learned that exhaustion was more reliable than persuasion. Most importantly, it learned that performance could substitute for accountability if it is confident enough and sustained enough.

This is how normalization begins—not with a catastrophe, but with insistence. Not with secrecy, but with confidence. Not with coercion, but with repetition.

Reality was not abolished.

It was exhausted.

This book begins here because this moment contained the logic of everything that followed.

Sharpiegate was not the scandal.
It was the signal.

PART I— PRACTICE ROUND

CHAPTER 1: CROWD CONTROL

Immediately after the first inauguration, the first lie was told.

What made the lie important?

It wasn't about policy, or power, or war. It wasn't about ideology or governance or the machinery of the state. It was about numbers. About space. About how many people showed up and how many didn't. About a photograph that existed and a reality that refused to cooperate.

Anyone who has ever been to Washington in January could have told you the truth before the factual images circulated. Cold air does not inspire crowds. Security checkpoints do not inspire lingering. Long walks across frozen ground do not encourage attendance. These are not partisan observations; they are physical ones. And yet, within hours of the inauguration, the country was told—confidently, forcefully, without qualification—that what it had seen was not what it had seen.

This was not a denial. Denial hesitates. Denial waits to see if the contradiction fades. This was a rehearsal.

The claim was not that the crowd was respectable, enthusiastic, or symbolically significant. It was not that the moment carried energy or historic weight. The claim was absolute. The crowd was the largest ever. Not "one of the largest." Not "comparable to previous inaugurations." Not "strong given the weather." Largest. Ever. Period. Full stop.

Reality was dismissed on a technicality.

And when reality pushed back—as it always does, quietly and relentlessly—the administration did not retreat. It doubled down. Then tripled. Then sent a press secretary into a room full of journalists to insist, angrily, that this was the truth and that disagreement itself was suspicious. The correction was not treated as clarification but as provocation.

That was the moment it became clear this presidency would not be governed by facts.

It would be governed by posture.

Crowd size was never the issue. Control was. The question was not how many people attended, but who had the authority to define what attendance meant. If something this visible, this trivial, this provable could be rewritten without consequence, then nothing else was off-limits. If people could be convinced—or at least pressured—to argue about something so small, they would not notice what came next.

The outrage cycle performed exactly as designed. Late-night jokes arrived on schedule. Social media fractured into predictable camps. Fact-checks were published, skimmed, shared, and forgotten. Everyone argued about attendance while power quietly settled into place. The moment passed, unresolved but absorbed.

This was the soft launch.

Because once you convince a segment of the population that photographs lie, you no longer need to win arguments. You only need to repeat yourself louder than everyone else. Volume becomes authority. Confidence replaces verification. Repetition substitutes for proof.

What struck me was not that people believed the claim.
It was how quickly they were asked to.

There was no transition period. No easing into unreality. No gradual blurring of the line between exaggeration and falsehood. The demand for acceptance was immediate, delivered with enough confidence that hesitation felt like disloyalty. To question the claim was not to disagree; it was to betray.

And that became the rule.

From that day forward, facts would be negotiable. Institutions would be optional. Apologies would be extinct. Every contradiction would be reframed as an attack. Every correction would be dismissed as bias. Every question would be treated as hostility.

The crowd was the test case.

And America passed—barely noticing it had taken an exam.

This moment mattered because it established a precedent: truth would no longer be something to discover, but something to defend. Evidence would not be weighed; it would be challenged for daring to exist. Authority would not be derived from accuracy, but from insistence.

The administration also learned something valuable that day. It learned that outrage could be managed. That ridicule could be endured. That facts, once politicized, lose their stabilizing force. And it learned that attention—even negative attention—could be harnessed to obscure more consequential moves.

The crowd size was small. The lesson was not.

Because if a government can insist on an alternate reality at the level of a photograph, it can do so at the level of policy. If it can redefine something everyone can see, it can redefine things most people cannot. And if citizens are trained to argue endlessly about the obvious, they will have less energy to confront the structural.

This is how normalization begins—not with catastrophe, but with triviality. Not with violence, but with insistence. Not with secrecy, but with performance.

The first lie did not seem important on the surface.

But that is precisely why it worked.

This was the beginning of the grab.

CHAPTER 2: NATO? NEVER HEARD OF HER

Alliances are complicated things.

They are built on memory, obligation, and mutual understanding that not everything can be reduced to a transaction. They rely on shared history, mutual risk, and the long, unglamorous work of trust maintenance. They exist not because they are always efficient, but because they are stabilizing.

Naturally, this one was treated as an expense.

When the President of the United States publicly questioned the value of NATO, it was not done quietly, carefully, or strategically. It was done the way one complains about a cable bill—loudly, vaguely, and with the assumption that someone else was getting a better deal.

The problem was not skepticism. Presidents had pressured allies before. The problem was framing. NATO was not discussed as a diplomatic architecture that had prevented global catastrophe for decades. It was discussed as a bad subscription service.

Why are we paying so much?

Why aren't they paying more?

Why are we even doing this?

These are questions you ask an accountant.

Not the free world.

The rhetoric reduced a complex, multilateral security framework into a grievance narrative. The implication was not that NATO needed reform, but that loyalty itself was conditional. History did not matter if the invoice felt unfair. Sacrifice did not matter if the return on investment could not be immediately quantified.

Watching foreign leaders react was like watching someone realize—mid-conversation—that the person they were speaking to had not read the same script. Nervous laughter filled the gaps. Careful smiles masked alarm. Long pauses appeared where translators stalled, as if hoping the sentence might improve if left unfinished.

This was not a negotiation. Negotiation implies a destination. This was improvisation.

And improvisation, when backed by nuclear weapons, lands differently.

What struck me was not the immediate threat to NATO itself—it had survived worse—but the signal being sent. Alliances, the administration was announcing, were provisional. Loyalty was transactional. Commitments were subject to mood and moment.

This was not a worldview.

It was a vibe.

And the vibe said: *If it doesn't benefit me today, why should I care about yesterday?*

That question echoed far beyond press conferences. Allies heard it and began hedging. Adversaries heard it and began testing boundaries. Americans—many for the first time—heard how fragile the architecture of global trust actually was.

Alliances do not collapse in explosions.

They erode in doubt.

Once doubt is introduced, reassurance becomes harder. Promises sound temporary. Guarantees sound negotiable. The cost of uncertainty is not paid immediately, but over time in hesitation, in miscalculation, in missed coordination.

What made this moment especially destabilizing was its casualness. These were not remarks delivered after a deep strategic review. They were offhand, repeated, and performative. The tone suggested that alliances were favors rather than obligations, and that leadership meant leverage rather than stewardship.

Foreign policy became less about shared security and more about dominance signaling. The goal was not to strengthen institutions, but to demonstrate personal authority over them. If allies appeared uneasy, that discomfort was reframed as proof of effectiveness.

Strength, in this framework, was measured by reaction.

But alliances are not built to flatter egos. They are built to survive them.

The long-term danger was not abandonment, but unpredictability. Partners could no longer assume consistency. Commitments sounded conditional. Silence began to replace trust.

And once trust erodes, it does not return quickly.

The lesson of NATO was not that alliances are weak. It was that they require care. And care is incompatible with governance by grievance. When international order is treated as a business deal, history becomes expendable, and stability becomes optional.

The damage, like most damage during this era, was gradual. It unfolded quietly, beneath the noise. But its implications were profound: the United States was signaling that its word could be renegotiated at any moment.

Doubt, once introduced, is very hard to renegotiate.

CHAPTER 3: GEOGRAPHY IS FAKE NEWS

The border is everywhere.
It is collapsing in Texas.
It is flooding Arizona.
It is invading cities thousands of miles away.
It is, somehow, both a line that must be sealed and a force that cannot be contained.

Donald Trump speaks of "the border" constantly, yet rarely describes it as a place.

It is not a location with coordinates, jurisdictions, and laws. It is not a system governed by statutes, treaties, and procedures. In Trump's language, the border becomes an atmosphere—a permanent emergency that floats wherever fear is needed.

This is not accidental.
The border, in Trump's rhetoric, is not geography.
It is emotion.
And when geography becomes emotional, facts become optional.

Trump's border narrative rarely includes specifics. He does not talk about sectors, ports of entry, asylum law, or international obligations. He does not distinguish between migrants, refugees, or visa overstays. He does not locate the border within the real terrain of deserts, rivers, courts, and agencies.

Instead, "the border" is invoked as a single, undifferentiated threat.
It is always "wide open."
It is always "out of control."
It is always "worse than ever."
The repetition is the message.

By refusing to anchor the border in actual geography, Trump transforms it into a rhetorical device rather than a physical reality. This allows him to move it at will. When fear needs to be activated in New York, the border appears there. When political pressure builds in Chicago, the border migrates north. When justification is needed for federal force or emergency powers, the border suddenly becomes omnipresent.

A place becomes a weapon.

This is what it means for geography to become fake news—not that maps are wrong, but that location no longer constrains narrative.

Trump's border language collapses distance. It erases jurisdiction. It dissolves legal process into urgency. By the time the public asks where the crisis actually is, the answer no longer matters. The crisis has already done its work.

This flattening serves power.

If the border is everywhere, then any action can be justified anywhere. Federal authority can be expanded. Emergency language can be deployed. Normal constraints can be dismissed as naïve. Resistance becomes a denial of reality rather than a disagreement over policy.

Geography stops being a check.

It becomes an accessory.

Trump reinforces this by treating borders as symbols of dominance rather than systems of governance. Walls are discussed as talismans—proof of strength—rather than infrastructure subject to engineering limits, legal challenge, and environmental consequence. The wall does not need to function. It needs to signify.

Function is secondary.

Image is primary.

This symbolic approach allows Trump to ignore inconvenient truths: that most unauthorized migration does not happen through remote desert crossings, that asylum law exists regardless of slogans, and that international cooperation affects outcomes more than spectacle.

Those truths are geographically grounded.

They are, therefore, inconvenient.

So, they are dismissed.

The border narrative also blurs legal geography. Trump routinely collapses the distinction between federal and state authority, between domestic enforcement and international obligation. Governors are pressured. Courts are framed as obstacles. Judges become enemies of "security."

Law is treated as terrain to be conquered, not a structure to be respected.

This rhetorical strategy creates confusion by design. When people cannot tell where authority begins or ends, they are more likely to accept force as clarity. Ambiguity becomes permission.

Trump does not need the public to understand the border.

He needs the public to feel surrounded.

Once surrounded, precision becomes irrelevant.

This same approach appears in Trump's broader treatment of place. Cities are spoken of as crime zones rather than communities. Foreign countries are reduced to caricatures. Regions are flattened into reputational shortcuts—good, bad, weak, strong.

The world becomes a stage set, not a map.

And when the world is a stage, the loudest voice controls the scene.

This chapter follows the Prologue intentionally. The Sharpie incident showed what happens when a single physical fact contradicts presidential authority. The border rhetoric shows what happens when an entire geographic concept is dissolved into narrative.

One is an episode.

The other is a governing method.

By treating geography as flexible, Trump removes one of the last constraints on power. Distance no longer protects. Jurisdiction no longer limits. Reality becomes something that must negotiate with assertion.

That is the danger.

Because storms will still arrive where physics sends them.

People will still move where survival requires.

Borders will still exist whether rhetoric respects them or not.

And when policy is built on geography that isn't real, the consequences land on people who are.

.

CHAPTER 4: DIPLOMACY, BUT LOUDER

Diplomacy traditionally operates in whispers.

Not because leaders are timid, but because nations are permanent. A careless sentence can outlive the person who says it. A single adjective can harden into a position. A public insult can become a private grudge that shapes cooperation for years. So, the grown-up version of power, at its best, learns restraint—not as politeness, but as strategy.

This presidency prefers megaphones.

Every comment lands with the subtlety of a dropped cymbal. Allies are scolded in public. Adversaries are praised in ways that leave the room blinking. Agreements are announced like trophies, then revised like afterthoughts. Clarifications arrive late, if they arrive at all. The diplomatic posture is not "quiet confidence." It is performance—loud enough to drown out detail, fast enough to outrun correction.

There is a belief—popular in certain circles—that bluntness equals honesty.

That saying the quiet part out loud is bravery. That tact is dishonesty in a suit. That if you offend everyone equally, you must be "telling it like it is." This belief is convenient because it lets people mistake disruption for courage. It's also profitable, because it turns governance into content. A headline doesn't need nuance. A clip doesn't need context. A chant doesn't need footnotes.

What this era proves is that volume isn't clarity.

Volume is cover.

When everything is loud, nothing is precise. When every statement is maximal, none are binding. Outrage becomes white noise. Allies stop reacting in public because reacting only feeds the cycle. Critics tire. Supporters cheer reflexively. And somewhere inside that chaos, accountability slips out the side door, wearing a disguise that reads: "It was just a joke," or "You took it out of context," or the all-purpose shield of our time: "That's not what he meant."

The diplomatic effect is not immediate collapse. It's erosion.

A relationship does not end the first time a leader insults an ally. It changes. It becomes cautious. It becomes conditional. Everyone starts speaking in the language of exit ramps. The most telling shifts are the ones that happen quietly: a delay in coordination; a reluctance to share intelligence; an "I'll get back to you" that used to be a "Yes."

In that way, public ridicule can do what private disagreements rarely accomplish: it teaches partners to anticipate instability.

When allies are corrected publicly, they learn to prepare for embarrassment. When agreements are framed as favors, they learn to prepare for withdrawal. When commitments are treated as bargaining chips, they learn to hedge. Hedging is the diplomatic version of locking your door. You don't do it because you hate your neighbor. You do it because you no longer trust the neighborhood.

The press often covers the loudest moments as if they are the whole story.

A tense handshake. A raised eyebrow. A microphone catching an insult. These make great television because they look like conflict, and conflict looks like drama. But diplomacy isn't theater. It's infrastructure. It's pipelines and permissions and access and overflight rights. It's boring, until it isn't. And "isn't" is the point where your grandstanding becomes someone else's crisis.

There is a specific kind of danger in treating diplomacy as a brand.

Brands must be protected at all costs, even when wrong. Brands do not apologize; they "clarify." Brands do not learn; they "pivot." Brands do not admit weakness; they "reframe." In a brand environment, admitting error feels fatal—even when error is obvious, even when correction would build trust, even when the stakes involve actual lives.

So, error becomes identity.

And identity becomes a trap.

When leadership cannot concede small mistakes, it becomes incapable of managing large ones. When every correction is treated as a threat, every expert becomes an enemy. Eventually, the administration is forced to choose between reality and pride, and pride wins because pride is the only thing that can be broadcast immediately.

This is why "Diplomacy, but Louder" is not merely style. It becomes method.

Insults become signals. Praise becomes leverage. Confusion becomes a tool.

Unpredictability is sold as strength. The theory goes like this: if no one knows what you'll do next, everyone will fear you. Fear, in this theory, produces obedience. It's a toddler's view of power—effective in short bursts, disastrous as a system. Because fear also produces distance. And distance produces alternatives.

Allies do not want to fear the United States.

They want to rely on it.

Reliability is not glamorous. Reliability doesn't trend. It doesn't go viral. It is the quiet habit of doing what you say you will do, even when cameras are off. Reliability is why agreements endure. Reliability is why crises can be managed without panic. Reliability is why your words carry weight.

So, what happens when reliability is replaced with spectacle?

Your words start to weigh less. Not because you speak less, but because you speak too much. Not because you are ignored, but because your statements are discounted. People begin interpreting your public comments as performance rather than commitment. They stop planning around what you say and start planning around what you might do, regardless of what you say.

That is a loss of influence disguised as dominance.

And it is not corrected by speaking louder.

The personal becomes political in this environment, as it always does when power is performed as personality.

Diplomatic decisions begin to look like preferences. Relationships begin to look like grudges. Allies are praised or punished based on flattery. Adversaries are elevated because antagonism makes for good TV. Meetings are framed as "wins" or "losses" as if global stability were a boxing match.

The public is trained to watch foreign policy like sports.

Who dominated the handshake?

Who looked strong?

Who looked weak?

Who "owned" whom?

This framing reduces complex international dynamics into emotional scoreboard politics. It becomes easier to sell, easier to defend, and harder to govern. Because the world does not operate on a scoreboard. It operates on consequences.

Consequences are not impressed by volume.

They are impressed by preparation.

Under megaphone diplomacy, the staff work becomes more frantic. Diplomats and national security officials spend time explaining statements that should never have been made. They spend time assuring allies that "it's not that bad." They spend time translating rhetoric into policy. Translation is exhausting. Exhaustion is expensive. And eventually, exhaustion becomes its own form of failure.

A quieter administration can sometimes say, "We were wrong," and move on.

A louder one cannot.

It must fight reality to preserve the performance.

So diplomacy becomes a posture contest with the world.

And the world is not a helpful sparring partner. It pushes back in ways that don't fit into a news cycle. It pushes back in markets, in cooperation, in intelligence sharing, in votes at international bodies, in the willingness to take risks alongside you.

This is the part that rarely makes headlines: the slow loss of good faith.

Good faith is not naive optimism. It is the assumption that your partner is speaking sincerely, even when you disagree. It is the belief that your counterpart is operating within a stable framework of reality. Good faith is what allows disagreement without collapse.

When diplomacy becomes loud performance, good faith becomes scarce.

And when good faith becomes scarce, every dispute escalates.

Because there is no longer a shared assumption that anyone is operating honestly. In that environment, misunderstandings become deliberate insults. Mistakes become provocations. Normal bureaucratic delays become conspiracies. The world becomes a hostile stage because you keep narrating it that way.

This chapter matters because it shows how governance shifts from stewardship to spectacle.

The megaphone is not just louder. It is flatter. It cannot carry nuance. It cannot transmit humility. It cannot convey the careful layered meaning that diplomacy requires. It can only broadcast certainty.

But certainty without precision is not leadership.

It is noise.

Diplomacy is not about winning the room.

It is about not losing the future.

And the future, as it turns out, has a long memory.

CHAPTER 5: FINLAND HAS A BROOM

Every presidency has a moment where the country laughs together.

Sometimes that laughter is relief—an absurdity in a heavy week, a harmless gaffe that reminds people their leaders are human. Sometimes it's a pressure valve, the collective exhale after yet another day of tension. Sometimes it's the kind of laughter you hear at a funeral when someone tells a story that shouldn't be funny, but it is anyway because grief is too big to hold without humor.

This is one of those moments.

Wildfires are devastating the American West. Communities burn. People lose homes, businesses, and decades of memory in a single night. Firefighters work until their bodies quit. Families flee through smoke with whatever fits in the back seat. The situation is complex, technical, and rooted in a combination of climate, infrastructure, land management, and long-term planning.

Naturally, the explanation offered is… Finland.

According to the President, Finland doesn't have this problem. Why? Because they rake their forests.

Not manage.

Not fund.

Not coordinate.

Not implement multi-year hazard reduction strategies.

Not update building codes.

Not increase firefighting resources.

Not improve evacuation planning.

Not address climate trends.

Not invest in power grid resilience.

Not rethink development patterns in fire-prone areas.

They Rake.

It lands like a cartoon solution to a real problem, like trying to fix a collapsed bridge with a motivational quote. The statement is so confidently delivered that it briefly breaks the listener's brain. People struggle to respond because the appropriate reaction is unclear. Do you laugh? Do you correct? Do you ask what, exactly, is being raked? Pine needles? Underbrush? Entire mountains? The whole idea is so small and so specific that it feels beneath serious rebuttal.

And that's the trick.

The smaller the claim, the harder it is to treat it with the weight it deserves. It feels petty to correct it. It feels humorless to take it seriously. It feels like overkill to explain forest management on national television. So, the public does what it always does when presented with absurd confidence: it makes jokes.

The internet blooms.

Memes appear instantly. Photoshopped Finns pose heroically with garden tools. Leaf rakes are christened as weapons of salvation. People make parody instructional videos: "Step one: rake the wildfire." Finland's officials—polite, baffled, Scandinavian to the core—clarify that no, the nation is not saved by a national leaf-removal program. Professional foresters and scientists attempt to explain that Finland does have forest management practices, yes, but not the cartoon version being broadcast.

In a normal administration, this would end here.

A joke. A footnote. A late-night monologue. A "whoops" followed by an actual discussion of policy.

But this administration does not treat ridicule as a warning sign.

It treats it as engagement.

Laughter becomes data. Outrage becomes oxygen. If the country is talking, the machine is winning. The goal is not to be correct; it is to be central. Not to solve the problem; it is to dominate the conversation about the problem.

That is why "Finland has a broom" matters.

The problem isn't the rake. The problem is the instinct behind it: complex realities reduced to simple metaphors delivered with confidence so absolute that correction seems rude. The metaphor is not offered as one idea among many; it is offered as the idea, the definitive answer that separates the "common sense" people from the "overthinking" people.

This is not misinformation in the accidental sense.

It is mythmaking.

And myths do not need to be true.

They need to be memorable.

A myth has an emotional shape. It gives people something to repeat at dinner. It offers an image they can carry: forests neatly cared for, problems solved by simple effort, a foreign country demonstrating discipline the home country allegedly lacks. It converts the messy complexity of climate and policy into a moral narrative: we suffer because we are lazy; others thrive because they are tidy.

That narrative is intoxicating.

It is also false.

But false narratives can be useful. They redirect blame away from leadership and toward the public. They imply that if you disagree, you are making excuses. They replace structural analysis with personal shame. If only Californians raked harder, the story suggests, they would stop burning.

This is what makes the joke dangerous.

It packages a policy failure as a personality flaw.

The administration can then position itself as the voice of "common sense," even while refusing the complex work that real solutions require. It can dismiss experts as pessimists and bureaucrats as obstacles. It can frame investment as waste and planning as cowardice. The myth allows leadership to speak confidently without governing competently.

And the public response—laughing, sharing memes, making jokes—becomes part of the cycle.

Comedy, in this administration, is camouflage.

People laugh, but they also learn something: policy will arrive disguised as punchlines. If you challenge it, you are "taking it too seriously." If you insist on details, you are an elitist. If you ask for evidence, you are "triggered." The burden shifts. The person demanding accuracy becomes the problem. The person selling fiction becomes "authentic."

It is a clever inversion.

And it is exhausting.

This chapter is not written to scold people for laughing.

We all laughed, or at least we wanted to. Because the alternative was to sit with the truth: that leadership was offering cartoon solutions to real suffering and doing it with pride. Humor was not a moral failure. It was a coping mechanism.

But coping mechanisms become dangerous when they replace accountability.

The joke fades. The fires continue. People rebuild. Others do not. Insurance systems strain. Infrastructure debates resume. Climate trends worsen. The problem persists because it is larger than any one season and more complicated than any one metaphor.

And then the next absurd statement arrives.

And the cycle repeats.

That is why this chapter belongs in a recall-all, instead of a tell-all.

Not because "raking the forest" is the worst thing said.

But because it is the perfect illustration of how the era works:

Reduce complexity.

Replace policy with performance.

Turn correction into conflict.

Turn ridicule into engagement.

Move on.

A nation cannot solve wildfires with a rake.

But it can avoid responsibility with a punchline.

And that, in this era, is often the point.

CHAPTER 6: EVERYONE'S A WITCH

At some point, criticism stops being disagreement and becomes a conspiracy.

Investigations are no longer legal processes; they are "witch hunts." Judges are no longer neutral; they are biased. Journalists are no longer skeptical; they are enemies. Experts are no longer informed; they are compromised. The vocabulary narrows until everything fits into two categories: loyal or illegitimate.

Once that vocabulary takes hold, governance changes.

The phrase "witch hunt" is not clever because it is accurate. It is clever because it is cheap. It costs nothing. It requires no evidence. It rejects the premise that evidence matters. It is a rhetorical shortcut that converts accountability into persecution and transforms scrutiny into villainy.

A witch hunt is never designed to find witches.

It is designed to make everyone afraid of being accused.

That is the mechanism.

When the President calls an investigation a witch hunt, supporters are invited to see themselves as part of a besieged tribe. Critics are cast as persecutors. Institutions become tools of oppression. The state is not doing its job; it is "targeting" a person unfairly. The public is encouraged to choose a side before any facts are examined, because the facts will be framed as weapons anyway.

This does two things at once.

First, it inoculates the audience against bad news. Any evidence that emerges can be dismissed as manufactured. Any testimony can be recast as coerced. Any legal outcome can be framed as political. This is not a defense in court; it is a defense against reality.

Second, it deters participation in accountability itself. Witnesses become traitors. Investigators become villains. Civil servants become "deep state." People who might otherwise cooperate become reluctant, not because they lack integrity, but because they can see the social cost of being labeled an enemy. The label is sticky. It follows you. It attracts threats. It stains careers.

Fear becomes policy.

The chilling effect is not accidental.

It is functional.

Slowly, the question in public discourse shifts.

It shifts from "Is this true?" to "Is it worth responding?"

From "What happened?" to "Who benefits?"

From "What does the evidence show?" to "Which team are you on?"

These shifts are corrosive because they transform a system designed for verification into a culture designed for allegiance.

Institutions begin to bend—not always because they believe the narrative, but because they are exhausted by it. Every clarification becomes a fight. Every correction becomes a headline. Every attempt at neutrality becomes an invitation to be attacked from both sides. The reward for doing your job becomes harassment. The punishment for speaking is personal risk.

So, people speak less.

And when they do speak, they speak cautiously.

Caution is then framed as guilt.

This is how the trap works: if you defend yourself, you "prove" you're part of the conspiracy. If you ignore it, you "prove" you have something to hide. If you cooperate, you're a rat. If you refuse, you're obstructing. There is no action that is not interpreted as guilt because guilt is not determined by facts. It is assigned by narrative.

The "witch hunt" story also has a convenient secondary effect: it keeps the leader at the center of the story.

An investigation is not just something happening. It is something happening to him. The news cycle becomes a daily episode of victimhood and defiance. Supporters are mobilized not around policy achievements, but around personal grievance. Politics becomes therapy—an endless group session where anger is validated, suspicion is rewarded, and institutions are scapegoated for discomfort.

In this environment, loyalty becomes the primary currency.

Not competence.
Not integrity.
Not consistency.
Just loyalty.

Once loyalty becomes the measure of legitimacy, everything else becomes suspect. Officials are evaluated not by whether they enforce the law, but by whether they protect the leader. Judges are evaluated not by whether they follow precedent, but by whether they deliver favorable outcomes. Journalists are evaluated not by whether they report accurately, but by whether they flatter.

This is why the "witch hunt" era matters beyond any single investigation.

It introduces an authoritarian instinct into a democratic culture: the idea that accountability is persecution and that the only legitimate institutions are the ones that serve the leader's interests.

It also trains the public to distrust the very mechanisms designed to protect them.

Courts. Elections. Agencies. Inspectors. Auditors. Scientists.

All of it becomes "rigged" if it contradicts the narrative.

When people are trained to distrust institutions, they become easier to manipulate.

Because if the referee is corrupt, then any outcome can be dismissed. If the scoreboard is fake, then losing doesn't count. If the doctor is lying, then the illness is a rumor. If the scientist is compromised, then reality is propaganda. Skepticism becomes the gateway drug to cynicism, and cynicism becomes the foundation for control.

This shift doesn't happen overnight.

It happens through repetition.

The phrase "witch hunt" is repeated until it becomes a reflex. A headline appears and the reflex fires: witch hunt. A subpoena is issued, and the reflex fires: witch hunt. A witness speaks, and the reflex fires: witch hunt. The words become a noise that replaces thought. Repetition does not prove a claim, but it can drown out questions.

And when questions drown, power rises.

There is also something emotionally comforting about the witch hunt story.

It offers simplicity. It offers villains. It offers certainty. It offers a clear moral structure: the leader is innocent, the critics are malicious, the system is unfair. Complexity is reduced to persecution. Any discomfort can be explained as oppression. The story supplies meaning in a world where meaning is scarce.

That emotional comfort is costly.

Because democracy requires discomfort. It requires that leaders be questioned. It requires that institutions function even when they are inconvenient. It requires that people tolerate outcomes they don't like, trusting that the process is still worth defending.

The witch hunt narrative attacks that tolerance.

It teaches people that losing is illegitimate.

That correction is hostility.

That disagreement is betrayal.

That accountability is oppression.

In the long run, this is more damaging than any one scandal, because it reshapes the public's relationship with truth itself.

A society can survive scandal.

It cannot survive the death of shared reality.

By the time "everyone's a witch" becomes the default frame, the culture has already shifted. People no longer argue about facts. They argue about loyalties. They no longer ask, "What happened?" They ask, "Who are you with?"

And that is the point.

Because once every critic is an enemy and every institution is biased, the leader becomes the only trusted source of truth.

A president becomes a prophet.

A party becomes a church.

And doubt becomes heresy.

This chapter is written as a warning disguised as a description.

When a nation begins treating accountability as persecution, it is not simply defending a leader.

It is dismantling the tools that would protect it from the next one.

Witch hunts do not end with witches.
They end with silence.

CHAPTER 7: SHARPIEGATE

Some events are not scandals because of what happened.

They are scandals because of what didn't happen afterward.

The Sharpie incident should have ended in minutes. An incorrect statement about a hurricane's projected path is corrected by experts. A clarification is issued. The public moves on. This is the muscle memory of functional governance—error, correction, resolution.

Instead, it becomes a campaign.

What began as a single altered map metastasizes into a multi-day insistence that the alteration was justified, that the experts were wrong, and that the correction itself was the real offense. The issue is no longer meteorology. It is authority.

And authority cannot be wrong.

The Sharpie remains not because it matters, but because removing it would concede something far more dangerous to the governing style of this era: that reality has veto power.

This is where Sharpiegate stops being an anecdote and becomes doctrine.

The administration's response is not passive. It is active resistance to correction. Agencies are pressured. Statements are massaged. Language is carefully chosen to avoid contradiction without admitting error. Bureaucracy bends—not because it agrees, but because it is trapped.

Career officials find themselves in an impossible position. Their job is to communicate accurate information that protects the public. Their boss has publicly committed to a falsehood. Correcting it now is framed as insubordination. Remaining silent is framed as complicity.

This is the real scandal.

Not the marker.

Not the map.

But the coercion of institutions into performing loyalty rather than truth.

Sharpiegate reveals how power functions when it cannot retreat. The moment correction becomes political, accuracy becomes negotiable. Expertise becomes optional. Agencies become props in a performance designed to preserve dominance at all costs.

The weather service releases statements that read like riddles. Language twists itself into knots to avoid saying what everyone already knows. The forecast is restated without restating the correction. The implication is clear: truth must now pass through a filter of approval.

This filter reshapes everything.

Once institutions learn that accuracy can be punished, they begin pre-editing reality. They anticipate reactions. They soften conclusions. They delay releases. None of this requires an explicit order. The pressure is ambient. Everyone understands the stakes.

This is how authoritarian instincts spread in democratic systems: quietly, procedurally, through risk management.

No one says, "Lie."

They say, "Be careful."

No one says, "Change the facts."

They say, "Think about how this will land."

Sharpiegate becomes a template.

From that moment on, correction is treated as confrontation. Expertise is viewed as a challenge. Institutions are expected to protect the narrative, not the public. The marker line becomes symbolic—a literal drawing over reality to make it comply.

The public response is fragmented.

Some people are alarmed. Others are amused. Many are simply tired. The spectacle absorbs attention without producing resolution. As with the crowd size lie, survival replaces accountability. The story fades without closure.

But the lesson remains.

The lesson is that error does not require correction if it can be defended long enough. That exhaustion is a strategy. That if you hold the line, reality will eventually get bored.

This lesson is applied repeatedly.

From public health guidance to election integrity to international relations, the same pattern emerges. An assertion is made. Experts contradict it. The contradiction is framed as hostility. Institutions hesitate. The assertion survives.

Sharpiegate never ends because it is no longer about the Sharpie.

It is about narrative sovereignty.

Who gets to decide what is real?

Who has the authority to define truth publicly?

Who is allowed to correct whom?

In previous administrations, these questions were boring. The answers were assumed. Facts belonged to institutions. Leaders responded to them. Disagreement existed, but correction was expected.

That expectation collapses here.

Reality becomes adversarial.

The administration does not merely reject the correction; it retaliates against it. Officials who clarify are sidelined. Agencies are warned. The message is unmistakable: loyalty is measured by silence.

Silence spreads.

Experts retreat from public explanation. Scientists choose their words carefully. Reports are delayed. Briefings are sanitized. The public sees less clarity, not because clarity is unavailable, but because it is unsafe.

This is the chilling effect of Sharpiegate.

It teaches institutions that even obvious truths can be dangerous if they contradict power. It trains public servants to weigh personal risk against professional duty. It redefines leadership as dominance over facts rather than stewardship of them.

The international community notices.

Allies observe how easily internal expertise is overridden. Adversaries observe how readily confusion can be generated. Both adjust accordingly. Confusion becomes a feature, not a bug.

This has consequences.

When the United States appears unable—or unwilling—to align its public statements with observable reality, its credibility erodes. Not catastrophically, but incrementally. Each incident adds weight. Each contradiction chips away.

Sharpiegate adds a significant chip.

Because it is so small.

It demonstrates that if leadership cannot concede a minor, harmless error, it cannot be trusted to concede larger, consequential ones. If it will fight a weather map, it will fight anything.

The public absorbs this too.

People begin to understand that arguing facts is pointless. They shift to arguing motives. They stop expecting correction. Cynicism grows. Trust declines.

Democracy becomes theater.

Sharpiegate is also revealing because of its sheer absurdity. The fact that something so trivial becomes a multi-day controversy is itself a warning sign. Systems that are healthy do not fixate on markers. Systems under strain do.

The marker becomes a loyalty test.

Do you accept the altered map?

Do you question it?

Do you stay silent?

These questions divide people not by knowledge, but by allegiance. The act of acknowledging reality becomes political.

This is not governance.

It is conditioning.

By the time Sharpiegate faded, the damage was done. The precedent was set. Reality can now be negotiated publicly. Institutions can now be pressured into ambiguity. Correction can now be framed as betrayal.

The marker is gone.

The lesson remains.

Sharpiegate never ends because it reappears in every subsequent conflict between fact and power. It echoes in public health briefings. It resurfaces in election disputes. It shadows court decisions. The outline changes. The method does not.

Draw over reality.

Defend the drawing.

Punish the eraser.

This chapter matters because it marks the point where error became policy and insistence became governance. It shows how a moment of absurdity evolved into a mechanism of control.

A democracy can survive mistakes.

It struggles to survive the refusal to admit them.

Sharpiegate is not about a storm.

It is about whether truth is allowed to exist independently of power.

And once that question is asked, it never really goes away.

CHAPTER 8: PANDEMIC CONFIDENCE

Viruses do not care about confidence. There are moments when confidence is reassuring.

A steady voice in a storm can calm panic. A composed demeanor can prevent chaos. Leadership, at its best, communicates resolve without denying uncertainty. It tells the truth without amplifying fear. It understands that credibility, once lost, is almost impossible to regain.

This moment required that kind of confidence.

What it received instead was a performance.

The crisis arrived quietly at first. Reports trickle in. Warnings were cautious. The language was clinical, almost dull. It sounded distant—something happening elsewhere, something that experts were monitoring. This distance created a dangerous comfort. Since the problem was far away, it felt manageable. If it feels manageable, urgency can wait.

Waiting became the strategy.

Public statements were optimistic. The situation was "under control." The threat was "very low." Reassurance was delivered without context, without caveat, without preparation for the possibility that reassurance might have been wrong. Certainty was offered not as a hypothesis, but as a declaration.

Confidence took the stage before competence arrived.

Experts urged caution. They recommended preparation, testing, coordination, and transparency. These suggestions were not dramatic. They were procedural. They required logistics, funding, and time. They did not translate easily into applause.

Confidence did.

The administration embraced the tone of inevitability. The problem would "disappear." It would "go away." The language was absolute, almost magical. The implication was not that work is being done, but that work would not be necessary.

This was not reassurance.

It was denial dressed as optimism.

Denial is seductive because it offers relief without cost. It allows people to believe that normalcy can be preserved without sacrifice. It allows leadership to avoid hard conversations. It postpones accountability.

The public wanted to believe it.

Early on, many did. The desire for normalcy was powerful. It competed easily with abstract warnings. The absence of visible impact reinforced the narrative. If nothing bad has happened yet, perhaps nothing will.

Perhaps this was all overblown.

The administration reinforced this hope. Contradictory statements were smoothed over. Numbers were minimized. Comparisons were made that reduced the perceived threat. The emphasis was on confidence, not readiness.

Readiness would require admission.

Admission that the system was strained.

Admission that mistakes are possible.

Admission that expertise matters.

Those admissions did not arrive.

Instead, public briefings became showcases of certainty. Predictions were offered without evidence. Treatments were discussed casually. Scientific nuance was flattened into soundbites. The line between hope and fact blurred.

This blurring was costly.

When leadership spoke with unwarranted certainty, it created expectations that reality couldn't meet. Each unmet expectation eroded trust. Each contradiction forced recalibration. The public learned to discount official statements—not because they were always wrong, but because they were unreliable.

Reliability matters most in a crisis.

The tone of confidence also pressures institutions. Agencies are encouraged to align messaging with optimism. Data releases are framed carefully. Language is massaged to avoid alarm. The appearance of control becomes a priority.

Control, however, cannot be announced into existence.

Behind the scenes, preparation lagged. Testing was slow. Coordination faltered. Supplies ran short. The gap between rhetoric and reality widened. When the impact became undeniable, the shift was abrupt.

Confidence collapsed into confusion.

The administration pivoted without acknowledgment. Earlier statements were ignored. New explanations emerged. Responsibility diffused. The narrative fractured. The public was left to reconcile contradictory messages on their own.

This reconciliation was exhausting.

People attempted to follow guidance that changed without explanation. They heard assurances alongside warnings. They watched leaders model behavior that contradicted recommendations. The signal became noise.

Noise undermined compliance.

Public health depends on trust. People must believe that guidance is based on evidence, not convenience. When trust erodes, adherence becomes selective. Individuals choose which rules to follow based on personal interpretation rather than collective need.

This is not rebellion.

It is confusion.

The administration's confidence continued even as evidence mounted. Numbers were questioned. Methodologies were disputed. Experts were sidelined or contradicted publicly. The performance persisted because retreat would require admission—and admission would puncture the image of certainty.

Certainty became the brand.

The problem with branding a crisis is that reality does not respect branding guidelines. It does not wait for messaging approval. It does not adjust its behavior to fit narratives.

Reality arrives anyway.

Hospitals strained. Workers fell ill. Families grieved. The consequences that were deferred become unavoidable. The earlier confidence now looked reckless. The gap between what was promised and what occurred became visible.

At this point, blame entered.

Responsibility shifted outward. States were faulted. Institutions were criticized. Experts were accused of inconsistency—the narrative reframed failure as betrayal rather than miscalculation.

This reframing preserved the performance.

If the problem was someone else's fault, the confidence could remain intact. If the system failed because it was sabotaged, rather than being unprepared, then the brand could survive.

The cost was cohesion.

Public health became politicized. Basic precautions became identity markers. Guidance was filtered through allegiance. The virus did not care, but the response did.

The administration insisted that it was following the science while contradicting scientists. It praised experts selectively and publicly undermined them when it was inconvenient. The mixed signals intensified.

The public learned a dangerous lesson: expertise is optional.

This lesson extends beyond the crisis. Once people are trained to doubt experts during emergencies, that doubt persists. Skepticism hardens. Trust fractures. The next warning arrives to a more resistant audience.

Pandemic confidence leaves scars.

This chapter matters because it shows how tone can shape outcomes. Leadership does not need to know everything in a crisis. It needs to be honest about what it does not know. Confidence is not the enemy. Overconfidence is.

Overconfidence prevents preparation.

It delays response.

It punishes correction.

The insistence on certainty transforms uncertainty into shame. Admitting doubt becomes weakness. Asking questions becomes disloyal. The culture of inquiry collapses under the weight of performance.

The public is not fooled indefinitely.

As reality asserts itself, the earlier assurances are remembered. Trust is not destroyed in one moment; it is depleted over time. Each contradiction draws from the reserve. Eventually, the account runs dry.

When trust is gone, compliance becomes coercion.

Rules must be enforced rather than followed. Guidance must be policed rather than accepted. The social fabric strains. Division deepens.

The tragedy is not that leaders tried to reassure. Reassurance is human. The tragedy is that reassurance replaced preparation, and confidence replaced competence.

Competence is quieter.

It plans.

It coordinates.

It listens.

It adapts.

Confidence, when unmoored from competence, is a liability. It feels good. It sounds strong. It photographs well. But it does not save lives.

This chapter closes with a simple observation: crises do not reward bravado. They reward humility. They reward systems that can learn publicly, correct quickly, and speak honestly—even when the truth is uncomfortable.

Pandemic confidence offers comfort without capacity.

And when capacity is what is required, comfort becomes cruelty.

CHAPTER 9: BALLOTS GONE WILD

Democracy depends on losing.

That sentence makes people uncomfortable, but it is true. A functioning democratic system assumes that every side will eventually lose something—an election, a vote, a policy fight—and that the loss will be accepted as legitimate even when it is painful. The system survives not because everyone wins, but because everyone agrees to keep playing after they lose.

This agreement is fragile.

It is not enforced by force. It is sustained by norms, repetition, and trust. People accept outcomes not because they like them, but because they believe the process was real. Once that belief is undermined, democracy does not collapse immediately. It wobbles. It becomes noisy. It begins to creak under the weight of suspicion.

President Trump's first administration learned how powerful that suspicion could be.

Long before any ballots were cast, the groundwork was laid. Elections were described as "rigged." Systems were "corrupt." Officials were "incompetent" or "partisan." These claims were not attached to evidence; they were attached to emotion. They were repeated often enough to feel familiar, and familiarity breeds acceptance.

The key was timing.

The accusations arrived early, before outcomes were known. This ensured that any unfavorable result could be framed not as a loss, but as theft. The narrative did not need to change based on facts. It was already in place.

Ballots were not yet counted.

The verdict was already written.

This was not skepticism.

Skepticism asks questions.

This was preemptive disbelief.

The administration insisted it was merely raising concerns. That vigilance protects democracy. That questioning systems strengthened them. In theory, that was true. In practice, the questions were not designed to improve integrity. They were designed to erode confidence.

The distinction matters.

When concerns are sincere, they come with proposals. They identify vulnerabilities and suggest remedies. They invite oversight. When concerns are strategic, they remain vague. They gesture broadly. They accuse without specifying. They spread doubt without offering solutions.

"Something is wrong" is more powerful than "Here is what to fix."

The public absorbs the message unevenly. Some people dismiss it as bluster. Others internalize it deeply. The repetition works. Trust does not evaporate; it thins. People begin to say things like, "I don't know what to believe anymore," which sounds neutral but functions as withdrawal.

Withdrawal is the goal.

When people disengage from shared reality, they become easier to mobilize emotionally. Facts lose their anchoring power. Evidence competes with narrative. Every report is suspect. Every authority is compromised.

The election approached under a cloud that did not need to exist.

Administrators, many of them career civil servants, prepared as they always have. Ballots were printed. Machines were tested. Procedures were followed. Safeguards were in place. The system did what it was designed to do.

But the narrative did not care.

Isolated errors were magnified. Normal delays were framed as malfeasance. Routine legal processes were portrayed as conspiracies. The complexity of election administration—always messy, always decentralized—is recast as proof of fraud.

Complexity becomes suspicious.

This framing is dangerous because elections are, by nature, complex. They involve millions of people, thousands of jurisdictions, and countless moving parts. Mistakes happen. They are corrected. This is normal. The system anticipates imperfection and builds in redundancy.

But redundancy looks like chaos if you are primed to distrust it.

The administration seized on this perception. Anecdotes replaced data. Claims circulated faster than corrections. Social media amplified confusion. The information environment fractured.

Officials attempted to reassure. They explained processes. They provided transparency. They invited observation. These efforts were sincere, but they struggled to compete with the certainty being delivered confidently.

Confidence won.

Once ballots were cast, the script was activated fully. Any outcome short of victory was framed as illegitimate. Legal challenges proliferated. Press conferences replaced evidence. Allegations multiplied.

The courts became a stage.

Cases were filed, not to be won, but to be seen. Losses were reframed as proof of corruption. Judges were attacked. Rulings were dismissed. The legal system was used not as an arbiter, but as a prop.

This strategy did not require success.

It required noise.

The noise keeps supporters engaged. It sustains anger. It converts disappointment into grievance. It prevents acceptance from taking hold.

Acceptance is dangerous to this model.

If people accept loss, the story ends. If they refuse, the story continues indefinitely. The election becomes an ongoing event rather than a concluded process.

This is how ballots "go wild."

Not because they are fraudulent, but because they are freed from finality. Every count becomes provisional. Every certification becomes suspect. Every safeguard becomes evidence of manipulation.

The concept of "proof" shifts.

Proof is no longer something demonstrated. It is something felt. If the outcome feels wrong, it must be wrong. Emotion outranks verification.

This inversion reshapes political identity.

Belief in the leader becomes incompatible with belief in the system. Loyalty requires disbelief. Doubt becomes virtue. Trust becomes betrayal.

The administration encouraged this binary explicitly and implicitly. Supporters were praised for "not buying it." Skeptics were mocked. Institutions were derided. The idea of a shared democratic outcome dissolved.

This dissolution had consequences.

Officials tasked with administering elections faced threats. Volunteers withdrew. Workers resigned. The machinery of democracy strained under the weight of hostility.

None of this was necessary to contest an election legally. All of it was effective at undermining confidence.

The most damaging aspect of this strategy was its persistence. Even after challenges failed, even after audits confirmed results, the narrative continued. The refusal to concede became a statement of strength rather than weakness.

Strength, in this context, means never accepting reality.

The public is left in a permanent state of uncertainty. People argue endlessly about what happened. They relitigate the same claims. The election never ends.

Democracy depends on endings.

Without them, governance becomes impossible. Policy stalls. Legitimacy erodes. Every decision is contested not on merit, but on origin. Authority becomes conditional.

This chapter matters because it shows how easily democratic trust can be weaponized against itself. The system's openness—its transparency, its decentralization, its reliance on good faith—is turned into a vulnerability.

Bad actors do not need to prove fraud.

They only need to suggest it convincingly.

Once doubt takes root, removing it is far harder than planting it. Corrections struggle to travel as far as accusations. Truth is slower than outrage. Verification is quieter than suspicion.

The long-term damage extends beyond one election.

Future contests are contaminated. Voters arrive already primed to distrust outcomes. Administrators operate under threat. Losers are encouraged to reject legitimacy as a matter of principle.

Democracy becomes conditional.

The administration frames this as patriotism. Questioning results is sold as vigilance. Refusal to accept loss is reframed as courage. The inversion is complete.

But courage in democracy looks different.

It looks like accepting outcomes you dislike.

It looks like defending processes even when they disadvantage you.

It looks like trusting institutions enough to lose.

Ballots do not go wild on their own.

They are set loose by leaders who refuse to let them settle.

This chapter closes with a warning disguised as observation: a democracy that cannot conclude its elections cannot govern itself. Suspicion, once normalized, does not remain targeted. It spreads.

And when every ballot is suspect, every future election becomes contested.

.

CHAPTER 10: WHEN WORDS WALK

For years, Donald Trump's words stayed on screens.

They appeared in tweets, speeches, interviews, and rally chants. They bounced across cable news and social platforms, amplified by outrage and defended by context. Supporters insisted he was speaking metaphorically. Critics warned he was being reckless. The debate itself became routine.

Words are cheap, people said.

Words are not action.

That assumption collapses after the 2020 election.

Trump does not merely dispute the outcome. He declares it stolen. He repeats the claim relentlessly, despite recounts, audits, court rulings, and certifications. The loss is framed not as defeat, but as betrayal. The system, he insists, has turned against "the people."

This chapter is not about free speech.

It is about what happens when presidential language becomes operational.

Trump's rhetoric did not remain static. It evolved. It escalated. It accumulated. What begins as a grievance hardened into a narrative, then into instruction. The transition was gradual enough to feel organic but deliberate enough to shape behavior.

First, enemies were named.

Election officials became villains. Judges became complicit. State authorities became corrupt. The press became an accomplice. Each accusation widened the circle of blame, ensuring that no single institution could fully resolve the grievance. If everyone were guilty, no outcome could be trusted.

Then the intent is assigned.

The election was not flawed—it was rigged. The loss was not procedural—it was criminal. Mistakes became malicious. Disagreement became treason. Trump did not argue that the system failed; he argued that it betrayed.

39

Betrayal demands a remedy.

Next, harm is defined.

Supporters were told that their votes had been erased, their voices silenced, their country taken from them. This is not disappointment; it is injury. Injury carried moral permission. Injury reframed aggression as self-defense.

Finally, a response was implied.

Trump did not need to issue explicit commands. He did not need to specify tactics. He only needed to insist that conventional remedies have failed and that strength is required. The implication filled the gap. The audience supplied the action.

Each step could be defended in isolation.

Together, they formed momentum.

Supporters gathered.

Grievances aligned.

A date was chosen.

January 6 did not arrive out of nowhere. It arrived on schedule.

Trump summoned supporters to Washington. He framed the moment as decisive. He told them the country is being stolen in real time. He insisted that weakness would lead to permanent loss. He urges strength. He urged presence.

When people arrived, they were not confused about why they were there.

They believed they were responding to truth.

This is the critical shift: language that once felt expressive now feels directive. The rhetoric that animated online spaces becomes embodied. The distance between belief and action collapses.

Words begin to walk.

The institutions tasked with anticipating this moment hesitated. Intelligence warnings existed, but they were fragmented and buried under noise. Responsibility diffused across agencies. No one wanted to overreact. Overreaction had been punished before. Caution felt safer than confrontation.

The result was paralysis disguised as restraint.

The day unfolded with a sense of unreality.

Crowds gathered where they were not supposed to. Barriers failed. Law enforcement was caught between restraint and confusion. The symbols of governance—chambers, desks, documents—were suddenly vulnerable in ways no contingency plan fully anticipated.

This was not a protest as a policy argument.

It was a performance of grievance.

Participants did not see themselves as rioters. They saw themselves as correctors. As patriots. As people acting on truths they had been told repeatedly by the most powerful voice in the country. The breach was framed as access. The violence was framed as a necessity.

Language had done its work.

Afterward, the reaction fractured predictably. Condemnation competed with minimization. Responsibility blurred. The words that built momentum were suddenly reframed as metaphor, exaggeration, and passion.

No one meant this, the argument goes.

This is not what anyone intended.

Intent becomes the refuge.

But outcomes do not care about intent. Institutions are breached. People are injured. Faith in democratic continuity fractures in full view of the world. The image of stability—the peaceful transfer of power, the durability of the process—absorbs damage that cannot be undone with statements.

The most dangerous response is not denial.

It is normalization.

Calls to "move on" arrive quickly. Fatigue sets in. The event is treated as an aberration rather than a culmination. Attention shifts. The cycle resumes.

But something fundamental has changed.

The boundary between speech and action is thinner now. The knowledge that presidential words can mobilize bodies, overwhelm systems, and alter history settles into place. The incentive to use language recklessly increases because the cost has proven negotiable.

This is not about censorship.

It is about responsibility.

Democracy relies on a shared understanding that language carries obligation—that accusations require evidence, that claims have consequences, that leaders bear responsibility for the climates they create.

When that understanding erodes, speech becomes a force without brakes.

Trump's defenders often retreat to a familiar argument: he did not *tell* anyone to do anything specific. But leadership is not judged only by explicit instruction. It is judged by foreseeable outcome. When a leader repeats a claim, escalates it, personalizes it, and frames conventional remedies as illegitimate, the range of plausible responses narrows.

At that point, action is no longer a surprise.

It is a feature.

This chapter matters because it marks the end of plausible deniability. The moment when rhetoric can no longer be dismissed as harmless. The point at which abstraction collapses and the physical world absorbs the impact.

Words walked.

And once they did, the country learned something it cannot unlearn: that belief, when repeated by power, does not stay contained. It migrates. It gathers. It acts.

The lesson is not limited to one man or one day.

It is structural.

If leaders learn that reckless language carries little cost, the temptation to use it grows. If supporters learn that action can be retroactively justified as passion, restraint weakens. If institutions learn that hesitation is safer than clarity, the next mobilization faces fewer barriers.

This is how democracies erode—not only through laws rewritten, but through norms abandoned. Through language untethered from consequence. Through the quiet acceptance that speech can be weaponized and then disowned.

Chapter 9 showed how systems bent.

This chapter shows how people moved.

Together, they explain why January 6 was not an anomaly, but a culmination—and why the conditions that produced it did not disappear simply because the calendar moved forward.

Words walked.

And they will again, if the lesson is not learned.

PART II— INTERMISSION

CHAPTER 11: STREAMING DEMOCRACY

Presidential power does not disappear when the office ends.

It migrates.

The transition is not abrupt. There is no clean handoff, no sudden silence. The platforms remain. The audience stays assembled. The language does not change. If anything, it becomes freer—less constrained by briefing rooms, more animated by grievance.

This is the moment when democracy goes on-demand.

The loss of formal authority is framed not as defeat, but as liberation. No more filters. No more handlers. No more obligation to reconcile words with policy. The performance can continue without interruption, and the audience—conditioned by years of spectacle—does not leave.

They subscribe.

Rallies resume quickly, now unburdened by governing responsibility. They feel looser, angrier, more theatrical. The speeches stretch. The grievances multiply. The applause arrives on cue. The language, sharpened by loss, becomes more expansive.

What once sounded provocative now sounds vindicated.

The platforms reward this evolution. Algorithms favor certainty over caution, outrage over explanation, repetition over nuance. The more extreme the claim, the farther it travels. The more aggrieved the tone, the stronger the engagement.

Democracy, once mediated by institutions, is now streamed directly.

The result is a strange inversion: the absence of office becomes proof of legitimacy. The loss is reframed as exposure. The narrative shifts from governance to persecution. Every legal challenge, investigation, or criticism is absorbed into a single storyline—*they are afraid of you because you speak the truth.*

This is not persuasion.

It is reinforcement.

The audience no longer needs convincing. They need affirmation. They need reassurance that their distrust was justified, that their anger was warranted, that their skepticism was prophetic.

And so the performance adjusts.

Facts become optional. Timelines collapse. Contradictions are reframed as evolution. Memory becomes selective, curated in real time. What matters is not coherence, but continuity of grievance.

This is how power survives without office—by occupying attention.

The infrastructure that once supported governance now supports spectacle. Media coverage persists because conflict persists. Outrage remains profitable. Silence is impossible because it leaves space for someone else.

The result is a permanent campaign state, unmoored from accountability.

Courts become stages. Depositions become content. Headlines become ammunition. Legal process is not addressed on its own terms, but as material for narrative expansion. Each development feeds the same loop: accusation, amplification, deflection.

Supporters are encouraged to see themselves not as citizens of a republic, but as members of a movement under siege. Loyalty deepens as distance from formal power grows. The leader no longer governs, but interprets—framing events, assigning meaning, distributing blame.

This is not the absence of power.

It is a different configuration.

Institutions struggle to respond. The traditional tools of accountability—fact-checking, rulings, reporting—feel mismatched to a system that does not require acceptance of outcomes. Decisions land, but belief does not follow.

The audience has been trained to treat unfavorable results as further evidence of conspiracy. Losses become proof. Constraints become confirmation. The system's resistance validates the story of persecution.

This is how democracy becomes content: endlessly produced, endlessly consumed, rarely resolved.

What makes this phase particularly destabilizing is its durability. Elections come and go. Laws change. Administrations rotate. But the attention economy does not reset. It carries grievances forward, preserving them in digital amber.

Nothing expires.

The effect on civic life is corrosive. Participation becomes performative. Engagement becomes reactive. Complexity collapses under the weight of narrative certainty. People stop arguing about policy and start arguing about reality itself.

And reality, when fragmented, cannot coordinate action.

This chapter matters because it explains how the first era does not end—it mutates. The loss of office does not quiet the movement; it intensifies it. Freed from institutional restraint, the performance sharpens.

The leader becomes a broadcaster.

The audience becomes an amplifier.

The system becomes a backdrop.

This is not a coup.

It is an occupation of attention.

The danger lies not in any single speech or post, but in the permanence of the loop. When democracy is experienced primarily through content, accountability becomes episodic. Outrage peaks and dissipates. Memory shortens. Fatigue sets in.

And fatigue is fertile ground.

By the time the return becomes possible—by the time the idea of restoration is floated—the audience is already primed. The narrative is in place. The grievances are organized. The system is framed as broken beyond repair.

The sequel does not arrive unexpectedly.

It arrives preloaded.

Streaming democracy teaches citizens to consume politics rather than participate in it. To watch rather than weigh. To react rather than deliberate. It transforms civic life into a series of episodes, each demanding attention but offering no resolution.

The applause never ends.

Neither does the anger.

This is where the first act closes—not with resolution, but with preparation. The audience is still seated. The stage is still lit. The language is still flowing.

The screen does not go dark.

It buffers.

CHAPTER 12: CAMPAIGNING FROM COURTROOMS

The courthouse is not built for performance.

Its architecture resists spectacle. Its language is procedural. Its rituals are repetitive and slow. Everything about it is designed to dampen emotion and elevate process. The court does not care who you are. It cares about what can be proven.

Which is precisely why it becomes useful.

As Trump's legal proceedings multiply, they are not treated as constraints but as content. Court dates are reframed as rallies by other means. Indictments are announced like tour stops. The language of accountability is translated instantly into the language of grievance.

This is not a defense.

It is repurposing.

The narrative arrives fully formed: the system is afraid. The timing is suspicious. The charges are political. Evidence is irrelevant because intent has already been assigned. Every summons is proof of persecution. Every motion is confirmation of a conspiracy.

The legal process is not engaged on its own terms. It is absorbed into a larger story that has been rehearsed for years—*they are coming for you, and I am in the way.*

The brilliance of this strategy lies in its inversion. Ordinarily, legal trouble weakens political standing. Here, it fortifies it. Each development becomes an opportunity to demonstrate resilience, to perform defiance, to reinforce loyalty.

Supporters do not ask what the charges are.

They ask who brought them.

And once motive replaces merit, outcomes no longer matter.

Court appearances are surrounded by cameras. Statements are delivered outside buildings designed to discourage statements. Silence is broken deliberately, because silence would allow the process to speak for itself—and the process is not trusted.

The law becomes a prop.

What follows is a familiar rhythm. Charges are announced. Outrage peaks. Donations surge. Poll numbers shift. Media coverage intensifies. The cycle repeats with mechanical precision. The courtroom does not interrupt the campaign. It feeds it.

This is campaigning from constraint.

The message to supporters is clear: the law is not neutral. It is a weapon. And if it can be used against me, it can be used against you. Loyalty becomes self-defense. Doubt becomes betrayal.

This framing does something profound. It collapses the distinction between individual accountability and collective identity. An indictment against one person is reinterpreted as an indictment against a movement. The courtroom becomes a battleground in a cultural war rather than a venue for adjudication.

And cultural wars do not require evidence.

They require allegiance.

Institutions respond as institutions always do—slowly, cautiously, with language calibrated to withstand scrutiny. But this caution is reframed as weakness. Precision is portrayed as evasion. Due process is described as a delay.

The public grows impatient, not because the system is failing, but because it is functioning as designed.

This impatience is cultivated.

Legal timelines are incompatible with the attention economy. Trials take months. Appeals take years. Evidence unfolds gradually. But the audience has been trained to expect immediate resolution. When resolution does not arrive, suspicion fills the gap.

Why is this taking so long?

What are they hiding?

Why won't they just admit it?

The answer—that law moves deliberately to avoid error—is unsatisfying in a culture conditioned by spectacle. Speed is mistaken for sincerity. Delay is framed as deception.

The campaign capitalizes on this mismatch.

Every pause becomes a talking point. Every procedural step becomes a grievance. The system's integrity is undermined not through attack, but through impatience. People are encouraged to feel wronged by the very mechanisms meant to protect fairness.

This is not a rejection of law.

It is a redefinition of it.

Law is no longer a standard. It is a tool. It is legitimate only when it produces favorable outcomes. When it does not, it is corrupt by definition. This conditional legitimacy hollowed institutions long before anyone noticed.

The effect ripples outward. Judges receive threats. Prosecutors are harassed. Court staff are vilified. The neutral machinery of justice becomes a target because neutrality itself is framed as hostility.

The chilling effect is real, but invisible. Cases are still filed. Rulings are still issued. The system continues. But the atmosphere changes. The cost of participation rises. The willingness to serve erodes.

And erosion is how systems fail—not through collapse, but through attrition.

What makes this phase distinct from earlier attacks on institutions is its efficiency. There is no need to dismantle the courts if you can discredit them. No need to abolish oversight if you can rebrand it as persecution. No need to win cases if losing them can be turned into fuel.

The campaign adapts seamlessly.

Fundraising emails reference court dates. Speeches frame legal language as a political attack. Supporters are urged to "stand strong" not against policy opponents, but against the system itself. The abstraction of "justice" is replaced by the immediacy of loyalty.

This strategy thrives on repetition. Each new case reinforces the last. The details blur together, which is convenient. Precision would require engagement. Vagueness allows emotion to lead.

Over time, the public stops distinguishing between allegations. Everything becomes part of a single narrative arc. The complexity of the legal system collapses into a single feeling: unfairness.

And unfairness, once internalized, demands remedy.

The danger here is not sympathy for the accused. Sympathy is human. The danger is the normalization of contempt for process. When courts are treated as obstacles rather than arbiters, the rule of law becomes conditional.

Conditional law is no law at all.

This chapter matters because it shows how accountability is neutralized without being abolished. The courts remain open. The judges still rule. The filings continue. But their authority is drained by narrative.

The campaign does not need to win in court.

It needs to win outside of it.

By the time verdicts arrive—whatever they may be—the audience is already insulated. Outcomes are dismissed. Appeals are promised. The story moves on.

The law is left behind, functioning but hollowed.

Campaigning from courtrooms works because it turns consequence into confirmation. It rewards defiance over reflection. It transforms accountability into ammunition.

And in doing so, it teaches a dangerous lesson: that power does not need to answer to law if it can persuade enough people that the law is the problem.

This is not the end of the story.

It is the staging ground.

Because once the courts are framed as enemies, there is nothing left to constrain ambition except public fatigue. And fatigue, after years of spectacle, is easy to manufacture.

The campaign continues.

The cases proceed.

The audience remains engaged.

The courtroom doors close behind the cameras.

Outside, the rally resumes.

PART III — THE SEQUEL

CHAPTER 13: BACK LIKE A RERUN

There is a difference between surprise and recognition.

Surprise arrives with a jolt. Recognition arrives with a sigh.

The return does not feel like a comeback. It feels like a resumption. The language is already familiar. The rhythms are already learned. The conflicts arrive prepackaged, their outcomes rehearsed. Nothing needs explanation. Everyone knows their lines.

That familiarity is the danger.

Trump's first time around, shock carried the energy. People argued intensely because the ground was shifting beneath them. Norms were broken loudly enough to trigger a response. Outrage felt urgent because the future felt undecided.

Now, the future feels repetitive.

Supporters greet his return with relief rather than exhilaration. Critics respond with fatigue rather than fury. Institutions prepare not with alarm, but with contingency plans refined by experience. The gasp is gone. The scroll continues.

This is how normalization deepens—not through acceptance, but through endurance.

Trump's governing style returns intact. Grievance remains the engine. Score-settling replaces agenda-setting. The language is less exploratory and more accusatory. There is no learning curve because learning is unnecessary. The posture has been validated by survival.

His return is framed as a correction. A restoration of rightful order. A vindication of patience. The past is recast not as disruption, but as interruption—something unfairly paused and now properly resumed.

That type of reframing matters.

If the first term could be treated as an anomaly, the second must be treated as confirmation. The behavior is no longer experimental. It is proven. It has endured scrutiny, scandal, loss, and return. It has outlasted condemnation.

Endurance becomes its own argument.

People who once promised vigilance now negotiate boundaries. This isn't because they approve, but because they remember the cost of resistance. Fatigue sets the limits. Attention narrows. The question shifts from *Should this happen?* to *How bad will it get this time?*

That shift is subtle, but decisive.

The administration understands this. The rhetoric sharpens accordingly. There is less need to persuade. The base is consolidated. The opposition is fragmented. The middle is tired. The audience has been trained.

The return is not about novelty.

It is about momentum.

What once required explanation now requires only assertion. Policies are announced with less preamble. Personnel decisions carry fewer justifications. Pushback is anticipated, absorbed, and dismissed before it forms.

The response cycle accelerates.

Criticism arrives.

Dismissal follows.

Attention moves on.

The machinery hums.

This chapter matters because it marks the end of plausible innocence. No one can say they didn't know what this would look like. The patterns are documented. The warnings were issued. The consequences were previewed.

And yet, here we are.

The danger of reruns is not unpredictability. It is complacency. When people believe they know how the story goes, they stop watching closely. Familiarity dulls vigilance. Repetition numbs urgency.

The administration benefits from this ambient exhaustion. Resistance feels repetitive. Alarm feels stale. Even legitimate concerns struggle to break through because they resemble earlier ones that did not stop the return.

The narrative of inevitability strengthens.

Institutions adapt by lowering expectations. What once triggered crisis meetings now triggers memos. Language is softened. Standards are reinterpreted. Survival becomes the goal rather than correction.

This is not a collapse.

It is an accommodation.

Accommodation feels pragmatic. It sounds responsible. It is often justified as realism. But over time, it rewires the system. Lines blur. Exceptions accumulate. Temporary measures harden into precedent.

The return exposes something uncomfortable: shock was never the solution. Shock only delays reckoning. What matters is sustained attention—and attention is hard to maintain when nothing feels new.

The rerun works because it exploits memory without learning. It relies on the audience remembering enough to recognize the scenes, but not enough to interrupt them.

Back like a rerun does not mean unchanged.

It means refined.

The edges are sharper. The grievances are more focused. The enemies are more clearly labeled. The playbook has been tested and adjusted. The vulnerabilities of institutions are known.

This is not nostalgia.

It is an iteration.

The chapter opens the sequel not with fireworks, but with familiarity. And familiarity, in politics, is one of the most powerful anesthetics there is.

CHAPTER 14: ACCELERATION WITHOUT CONSTRAINT

The sequel does not begin cautiously.

It accelerates.

What distinguishes Donald Trump's return from his first term is not novelty, but speed. The lessons of the past are not reconsidered; they are operationalized. Tactics that once tested boundaries now bypass them. Resistance that once slowed momentum now registers as background noise rather than meaningful friction.

The second act moves faster because it no longer needs permission.

Trump enters this phase with a refined understanding of where resistance lives and how to move around it. Institutions that once acted as brakes are now treated as obstacles to route around. Processes compress. Norms are dismissed in advance. Opposition is anticipated and neutralized rhetorically before it organizes.

Acceleration becomes governance.

In the first act, Trump encountered friction. Courts delayed initiatives. Bureaucracies slowed implementation. Advisors moderated impulse. The system absorbed pressure through drag. In the sequel, drag is treated as failure. Delay is framed as sabotage. Deliberation becomes disloyalty.

Trump no longer attempts to persuade institutions. He attempts to outrun them.

This shift fundamentally alters accountability. Oversight assumes time—time to investigate, to respond, to contextualize. Acceleration collapses that window. By the time objections surface, the action has already moved on, and attention has already shifted.

Speed becomes insulation.

The faster an action occurs, the harder it is to reverse. The quicker a policy is announced, the more it feels inevitable.

The sequel benefits from desensitization.

What once provoked outrage now competes with exhaustion. Each new provocation enters a crowded field of prior ones. Attention fragments. Reaction slows. Outrage cycles shorten. The system becomes reactive rather than anticipatory.

Trump exploits this lag.

He moves quickly not because the moves are careful, but because the system is tired. Fatigue replaces vigilance. Familiarity dulls urgency. The threshold for alarm rises with each repeated breach.

Acceleration feeds on lowered expectations.

When the public expects disruption, disruption loses its power to shock. The abnormal blends into routine. The extraordinary becomes procedural. Speed normalizes behavior that would once have required justification.

This dynamic reshapes institutional behavior.

Agencies preemptively adjust. Officials anticipate backlash rather than seek authorization. Risk tolerance shifts—not toward caution, but toward compliance. The safest posture becomes accommodation rather than resistance.

Compliance becomes adaptive.

The sequel also reflects a narrowed circle of influence. Trump surrounds himself with fewer intermediaries. Dissent is minimized. Loyalty is prioritized over expertise. Advisors are selected not for restraint, but for alignment.

Acceleration thrives in homogeneity.

Without internal challenge, decisions face fewer internal delays. Errors compound rapidly. Corrective feedback arrives late, if at all. Momentum replaces judgment. The pace itself becomes a justification: stopping would signal weakness.

Velocity substitutes for competence.

This is not efficiency.

Efficiency implies optimization—doing the right things with fewer resources. Acceleration implies motion—doing things quickly regardless of calibration. The two are often confused, but they are not the same.

Acceleration externalizes risk.

Consequences are displaced downstream. Policies roll out before impacts are assessed. Legal vulnerabilities surface after implementation. Human costs emerge after attention has moved elsewhere.

The system absorbs damage unevenly.

Institutions strain quietly. Individuals bear consequences disproportionately. Marginal populations experience disruption first. The appearance of decisiveness masks the absence of deliberation.

Trump's acceleration also relies on narrative preemption.

Actions are framed as inevitable before they occur. Opposition is portrayed as obstruction before it organizes. Debate is foreclosed by assertion. When outcomes are declared in advance, resistance feels futile.

This rhetorical acceleration compresses democratic space.

If decisions are framed as urgent, dissent appears irresponsible. If speed is equated with strength, hesitation becomes weakness. The tempo itself becomes a form of coercion.

Acceleration also erodes traceability.

Events blur together. Accountability fragments. It becomes difficult to isolate cause from effect. Each controversy is overtaken by the next. Memory compresses. The record becomes cluttered.

This clutter benefits speed.

When everything happens at once, nothing receives sustained scrutiny. The system struggles to assign responsibility because the timeline never stabilizes long enough for assessment.

Acceleration is not chaos.

It is directed overload.

Trump does not abandon control. He overwhelms response capacity. The system is not defeated; it is outrun.

Democracies are not designed for sprinting.

They rely on pacing—checks, pauses, review, and correction. Their strength lies in deliberation, not velocity. Acceleration without constraint destabilizes those rhythms.

The sequel does not announce this shift explicitly.

It enacts it.

Trump's governance style increasingly treats institutions as terrain rather than partners. Speed becomes a way to claim ground before opposition can organize. Each move creates new facts that must then be managed rather than debated.

The cost of this approach is cumulative.

Over time, institutions adapt by lowering standards. Procedures are streamlined beyond recognition. Safeguards are reinterpreted as inefficiencies. What begins as exception becomes practice.

Acceleration redefines normal.

This chapter extends the argument of Part II: repetition combined with speed creates vulnerability. The same behaviors, executed faster and with less resistance, produce greater impact.

The sequel is not more imaginative.

It is more efficient at bypassing limits.

That efficiency carries a price the system cannot indefinitely absorb. Acceleration without constraint does not immediately collapse democratic structures. It weakens them incrementally, testing how much strain they can tolerate before correction becomes impossible.

The danger is not a single sprint.

It is the refusal to slow down.

CHAPTER 15: LOYALTY AS QUALIFICATION

The sequel does not begin by changing laws.

It begins by changing people.

Donald Trump does not return to power asking what institutions require to function. He asks who controls them. Staffing becomes strategy. Appointments become enforcement. Loyalty is elevated from preference to prerequisite.

The lesson of the first act is clear: resistance lives inside institutions. Career officials delay. Advisors caution. Experts complicate. The sequel responds by removing friction at the source.

Personnel becomes policy.

Trump approaches staffing as filtration rather than recruitment. The goal is not to find the most capable individuals, but to identify the most reliable ones. Reliability, in this context, does not mean competence. It means alignment.

Alignment is not ideological consistency alone. It is personal fidelity.

This distinction matters.

In the first term, Trump repeatedly clashed with appointees who shared his political orientation but resisted his methods. Lawyers raised concerns about legality. Generals insisted on process. Civil servants cited statute and precedent. These frictions slowed execution, frustrated impulse, and exposed limits.

The sequel is designed to eliminate them.

Trump no longer treats expertise as an asset. He treats it as liability. Institutional knowledge becomes contamination. Experience becomes evidence of disloyalty rather than preparation.

This inversion reshapes the federal workforce.

Positions once filled through conventional vetting are now evaluated through loyalty metrics. Public statements, media appearances, social media activity, and even past silences are scrutinized. Prior dissent—however mild—becomes disqualifying.

Silence is safer than skepticism.

The result is not merely a change in personnel, but a change in culture. Individuals learn quickly what is rewarded and what is punished. Initiative narrows. Risk aversion increases. Self-censorship becomes routine.

The institution adapts not to serve the public, but to survive.

Trump's loyalty tests collapse the distinction between public service and personal service. Officials are expected to defend not only policy outcomes, but narrative framing. Disagreement is reframed as betrayal. Neutrality is treated as opposition.

This expectation travels downward.

Managers mirror the tone. Departments internalize the posture. What begins as presidential preference becomes organizational doctrine. The pressure to conform intensifies as it moves through layers of bureaucracy.

The sequel institutionalizes obedience.

This does not require mass firings or formal purges. It relies on signaling. Public firings, humiliations, reversals, and exclusions communicate boundaries more efficiently than policy memos ever could.

Compliance protects. Resistance exposes.

The chilling effect is cumulative.

When officials owe their positions to personal allegiance, incentives shift. They are less likely to challenge directives, flag risks, or document concerns. Records thin. Dissent disappears from internal channels.

Oversight weakens quietly.

The absence of objection is mistaken for consensus. Decisions appear smoother, faster, and more decisive. In reality, they are simply less contested.

This dynamic accelerates error.

Without internal friction, flawed policies move quickly. Corrective feedback arrives late or not at all. Consequences surface downstream, often after decision-makers have moved on.

Loyalty, once elevated above competence, becomes brittle.

Trump's approach also fractures institutional memory. Career officials depart. Expertise drains. Replacement hires lack context. The organization becomes easier to direct but harder to sustain.

Short-term compliance trades durability for control.

The sequel prioritizes immediacy over resilience.

Defenders frame this transformation as disruption. Bureaucracy, they argue, resists change. Efficiency requires decisiveness. Loyalty ensures execution.

But loyalty without competence does not produce efficiency.

It produces fragility.

Institutions stripped of internal challenge cannot self-correct. They fail abruptly rather than adapt gradually. They appear stable until stress reveals how hollow they have become.

This hollowness is not accidental.

Trump's governance style does not seek resilient institutions. It seeks controllable ones. Resilience requires autonomy. Control requires dependence.

Loyalty supplies dependence.

There is no single moment of collapse. There is accumulation.

Each replacement, each silence, each unchallenged directive shifts institutions slightly further from their purpose. By the time dysfunction becomes visible, the architecture that once corrected it is gone.

Personnel choices rarely make headlines.

Their consequences linger.

This chapter does not argue that loyalty has no place in governance. Shared goals matter. Trust matters. But when loyalty is personal rather than institutional, governance becomes precarious.

The sequel reveals this precariousness.

Trump governs as though institutions exist to validate authority rather than constrain it. Staffing decisions reflect that assumption. The result is a government that moves quickly, speaks confidently, and breaks quietly.

The sequel replaces friction with fidelity.

The question is not whether institutions can function this way briefly.

They can.

The question is how long they can function before failure becomes unavoidable.

Folders. Maps. Options arranged in columns. Risks circled. Probabilities debated. The point was not certainty but calibration—choosing among imperfect paths with eyes open to consequence. Decisions were meant to travel slowly because their effects traveled far.

This term prefers immediacy.

Announcements arrive before confirmations. Statements precede coordination. The posture comes first; the paperwork follows—if it follows at all. Foreign policy becomes something you feel rather than something you understand. Confidence replaces coherence. Mood substitutes for method.

It is policy by vibe.

The signals are loud and ambiguous at the same time. Strength is projected. Commitment is implied. Details are deferred. Allies scramble to interpret what has been said publicly before being told privately. Adversaries listen carefully, not for what is promised, but for what is omitted.

Diplomacy becomes atmospheric.

The administration treats unpredictability as leverage. If no one knows what comes next, the thinking goes, everyone must tread carefully. Uncertainty is framed as power. Surprise is marketed as strategy.

But uncertainty cuts both ways.

Allies need reliability more than bravado. They plan years ahead, align budgets, synchronize forces, and build public consensus on the assumption that words will hold long enough to matter. When signals fluctuate with tone, planning stalls. Hedging begins. Parallel arrangements are explored quietly.

None of this makes headlines.

It appears later—when coordination lags, when support arrives slower than expected, when trust thins without explanation. Foreign policy rarely collapses dramatically. It erodes through doubt.

What makes this phase distinct is its performative cadence. Statements are delivered with the assurance of finality, then walked back, then reframed as misunderstood. The audience is domestic as much as international. Applause at home is valued over clarity abroad.

Press conferences function like trailers. They tease impact without revealing plot. The language is cinematic: decisive, muscular, uncompromising. The mechanics remain offscreen.

And when mechanics intrude—when partners ask for clarification, when agencies seek alignment—the response is irritation. Process is portrayed as drag. Nuance is treated as resistance.

The result is a steady decoupling of words from outcomes.

Foreign policy by vibe relies on a bet: that confidence can outrun consequence. That tone can substitute for structure. That momentum can be sustained without scaffolding.

Sometimes it can—for a while.

Markets react instantly. Governments do not. They absorb shocks, recalibrate, and adjust. Over time, they learn how seriously to take signals. They discount bravado. They wait for follow-through. They build contingencies that assume inconsistency.

This is how influence shrinks without being announced.

The administration insists that respect has returned, measured by reaction. Coverage is constant. Statements trend. Leaders respond publicly. Attention is mistaken for alignment.

But alignment requires predictability. Without it, cooperation becomes transactional. Every ask is weighed for risk. Every promise is hedged.

The cost is cumulative.

Military planners adjust timelines. Intelligence sharing narrows. Diplomatic channels grow quieter as officials seek to avoid being blindsided by statements that will be interpreted as commitments they did not authorize.

The vibe travels faster than the policy. It outruns the people tasked with implementing it.

This chapter matters because it reveals a misunderstanding at the heart of this approach: foreign policy is not theater. It cannot be sustained by applause alone. The audience that matters most is not watching press conferences. It is watching follow-through.

And follow-through, when absent, teaches a lesson.

That lesson is not that the United States is weak.

It is that it is inconsistent.

Inconsistency invites testing.

Adversaries probe boundaries. Allies delay commitments. Neutral parties hedge. The system absorbs the uncertainty until something gives—usually at a moment when coordination would have mattered most.

Foreign policy by vibe feels powerful because it is immediate. It feels decisive because it is loud. But volume cannot replace architecture.

Architecture takes time.

Vibe takes a microphone.

The long-term effect is subtle but profound: the erosion of trust that does not announce itself until it is needed—and missing.

CHAPTER 16: GOVERNING BY PERMANENT CRISIS

The sequel does not promise stability.

It promises urgency.

Donald Trump does not govern as though crises are problems to be resolved. He governs as though they are conditions to be maintained. Emergency becomes atmosphere. Instability becomes leverage. The sense that something is always breaking, always threatening, always on the verge of catastrophe becomes the organizing principle of power.

Crisis is not incidental.

It is instrumental.

In conventional governance, crisis interrupts normal operations. It demands extraordinary measures. It justifies temporary suspension of routine. Trump reverses this logic. Crisis is not the exception; it is the baseline. Normal operations are framed as inadequate for a world that is always on fire.

This framing concentrates authority.

When danger feels constant, patience looks irresponsible. When a threat feels omnipresent, hesitation looks weak. Crisis collapses deliberation into reaction. It narrows choice. It rewards decisiveness over accuracy.

Trump thrives in this environment.

He speaks in absolutes. He identifies villains quickly. He simplifies causation. Complexity is dismissed as evasion. The goal is not to diagnose problems, but to dramatize them.

Dramatization mobilizes attention.

Each issue—immigration, crime, trade, public health, foreign relations—is presented as an existential threat rather than a policy challenge. The language of invasion, collapse, betrayal, and emergency saturates discourse. Fear sharpens loyalty.

Crisis creates permission.

Policies that would otherwise face scrutiny are framed as necessities. Oversight is delayed. Process is sidelined. The urgency of action crowds out questions about consequence.

The sequel intensifies this dynamic.

Trump no longer needs to introduce crisis narratives. They are already familiar. The audience expects danger. The infrastructure of alarm is in place. Each new claim fits seamlessly into an existing frame.

This continuity lowers resistance.

When everything is a crisis, nothing feels anomalous. The extraordinary blends into routine. The public becomes accustomed to heightened rhetoric without corresponding resolution.

Resolution is not the point.

Trump does not seek closure. Closure would dissipate urgency. Solutions would reduce leverage. Crisis must remain unresolved to remain useful.

This creates a feedback loop.

Crisis justifies authority. Authority generates action. Action produces disruption. Disruption confirms crisis. The cycle reinforces itself.

Institutions struggle to respond.

They are designed to manage discrete emergencies, not perpetual ones. They rely on escalation followed by de-escalation. Trump eliminates the second phase. There is no return to baseline because baseline is redefined as emergency.

This redefinition strains capacity.

Officials operate under constant pressure. Decision fatigue sets in. Burnout spreads. Errors increase. The system becomes reactive rather than strategic.

Trump benefits from this exhaustion.

A tired system is easier to dominate. Oversight weakens. Resistance fragments. Attention narrows to the most immediate threat, leaving long-term consequences unexamined.

Crisis also obscures accountability.

When outcomes are poor, blame is assigned to the crisis itself or to those accused of causing it. Failure is reframed as proof that the threat was real and the response insufficiently aggressive.

Escalation becomes the default answer.

This logic rewards overreach. If a policy fails, the solution is not reconsideration but intensification. The crisis narrative demands more force, more authority, more speed.

The sequel embraces this escalation.

Trump's rhetoric hardens. Compromise is framed as surrender. Restraint is depicted as negligence. Institutions that urge caution are cast as complicit in danger.

This delegitimizes dissent.

Critics are not merely wrong; they are irresponsible. They are accused of minimizing threat, aiding enemies, or undermining safety. The space for disagreement shrinks.

Crisis polarizes governance.

Trump positions himself as the sole actor willing to confront danger honestly. Others are portrayed as timid, corrupt, or compromised. This personalization of crisis consolidates loyalty.

Trust flows upward.

The leader becomes the solution to the crisis he defines. Dependence deepens. Institutions recede.

This chapter is not an argument that crises do not exist. They do. Societies face real dangers. But governing by permanent crisis distorts response. It prioritizes reaction over resilience.

Resilience requires calm.

Crisis consumes it.

The sequel reveals the cost of this approach. A government perpetually on edge loses capacity for foresight. It sacrifices durability for immediacy. It mistakes motion for progress.

The public absorbs this posture.

Citizens become habituated to alarm. Fear becomes ambient. Engagement becomes defensive rather than constructive. Trust erodes—not only in institutions, but in the possibility of stability itself.

The danger is cumulative.

A democracy conditioned to permanent crisis becomes brittle. It cannot absorb shock because it never recovers from the last one. It remains locked in emergency mode, unable to distinguish between genuine threat and manufactured urgency.

Trump governs comfortably in this environment.

The question is not whether crisis can mobilize action. It can. The question is how long a system can function when crisis is no longer episodic, but perpetual.

The sequel continues to trace this transformation: repetition creates familiarity, acceleration overwhelms response, loyalty filters dissent, and crisis justifies control.

The sequel does not collapse democracy outright.

It wears it down.

CHAPTER 17: FOREIGN POLICY BY VIBE

Foreign policy is supposed to be the part of government least dependent on personality.

Presidents come and go. Interests remain. Alliances outlast elections. Treaties are written precisely because the world does not have the luxury of improvising every four years. In a stable system, foreign policy is boring by design: predictable enough for allies to plan, clear enough for adversaries to calculate, and disciplined enough that crises do not become opportunities for auditions.

Donald Trump does not do boring.

Trump treats foreign policy less like a framework and more like a mirror. The world is not a map of interests; it is a stage for characters. The question is rarely, "What protects the long-term strategic position of the United States?" The question becomes, "Who looks strong? Who flatters? Who submits? Who humiliates? Who makes me feel respected?"

Foreign policy becomes vibe.

This does not mean there is no pattern. There is a pattern. It is consistent enough to predict, but personal enough to destabilize. Trump gravitates toward leaders who project dominance without apology and away from systems that require consultation, compromise, or shared constraint. He admires the posture of control, the aesthetics of force, and the simplicity of command.

That admiration shapes outcomes.

It shapes what is said in public, what is implied in private, and what allies and adversaries conclude about America's reliability. It shapes which crises are treated as moral emergencies and which are treated as transactional annoyances. It shapes who is portrayed as legitimate and who is portrayed as suspicious.

Vibe becomes a form of judgment.

And judgment becomes policy.

In the Trump era, the United States no longer speaks with one consistent voice abroad. It speaks with a mood that changes depending on the person in the room and the relationship Trump believes he is performing. The consequence is not always dramatic. Often it is subtle: a hesitation, a delay, an erosion of trust that does not announce itself, but accumulates.

Trust is not destroyed. It is depleted.

Foreign policy by vibe begins with a simple substitution: credibility is replaced by spectacle. A summit becomes a show. A handshake becomes a headline. A compliment becomes a bargaining chip. A snub becomes a national story.

The camera becomes the compass.

This is why the same posture repeats across different conflicts. Whether the issue is European security, Middle East war, or alliance management, Trump's instinct prioritizes dominance as performance. He is not most comfortable with diplomacy as negotiation. He is most comfortable with diplomacy as hierarchy.

Hierarchy produces clarity—at least emotionally.

Hierarchy also produces bias.

Nowhere does that bias feel more consequential than in Trump's posture toward Russia and Ukraine.

The question of Ukraine is, at its core, a question of sovereignty and deterrence. A sovereign nation is invaded or threatened, and the response of the world signals whether borders are rules or suggestions. Traditional American policy treats this as foundational: if aggression is rewarded, more aggression follows. If allies cannot trust commitments, they hedge. If deterrence weakens, conflict becomes more likely.

Trump's public posture toward Russia and Vladimir Putin repeatedly reads differently.

He speaks about Putin with a familiarity that feels indulgent. He frames Putin as "strong," "smart," "savvy"—a man who commands loyalty and controls his environment. Trump's language often carries admiration for Putin's clarity of command and the ease with which Putin consolidates authority. The admiration is aesthetic before it is strategic.

Ukraine, by contrast, is treated as a transaction.

Support is questioned as if it were charity. Commitment is framed as a burden. The moral clarity that typically accompanies an assault on sovereignty is replaced by suspicion—questions about motives, about corruption, about why the United States should "pay" for anything at all. The aggressor is afforded complexity; the victim is afforded doubt.

That asymmetry matters.

Because foreign policy is not only what is done. It is what is signaled. A leader's public posture communicates priorities. When an American president appears more comfortable praising an aggressor than affirming a victim, the signal travels.

Allies hear it.

Adversaries hear it.

Neutral countries hear it.

And domestic audiences absorb it too.

The message becomes: power deserves respect; vulnerability deserves skepticism.

Foreign policy by vibe does not ask, "Who is right?"
It asks, "Who looks like a winner?"

Ukraine does not fit Trump's preferred aesthetic. A democracy at war, dependent on allies, pleading for collective support—this reads as weakness in the Trump worldview. Putin's centralized command reads as strength. The strategic reality may be more complicated, but complication does not drive the vibe.

The vibe drives the frame.

This is not a small rhetorical issue. It reshapes deterrence. It suggests to authoritarian leaders that the United States might respond to aggression not with consistent opposition, but with negotiation shaped by personality. It suggests that flattery and dominance may purchase leniency.

It also destabilizes European partners.

When allies are unsure whether the United States views security commitments as obligations or as optional deals, they begin to plan differently. They invest differently. They coordinate differently. They hedge.

Hedging is not betrayal.

It is survival.

The same emotional architecture appears in Trump's posture toward Israel and Gaza.

The Israel–Gaza conflict is among the most complex moral and geopolitical challenges in modern foreign affairs. It involves legitimate security concerns, a longstanding history, trauma on multiple sides, and a humanitarian catastrophe when violence escalates. A serious approach requires nuance, restraint, and the ability to hold multiple truths at once.

Trump's vibe does not hold multiple truths well.

Trump's framing tends to prioritize a simple hierarchy: allies are defended, enemies are crushed, and any complexity that slows this binary is treated as weakness. Israel is embraced reflexively as an ally whose use of force is treated as self-defense almost by definition. The language emphasizes strength, retaliation, and victory.

Gaza, meanwhile, is discussed primarily through suspicion and dehumanizing generalities.

Civilian suffering becomes background. Humanitarian concern is framed as a distraction. The disproportionate power dynamics that make civilian casualties predictable in dense urban conflict are rarely held with seriousness. The vibe favors domination over deliberation.

This is not careful statecraft.

It is emotional alignment.

Foreign policy by vibe also reduces international conflict into domestic culture war symbols. Israel becomes a marker of "strength." Gaza becomes a proxy for arguments about protest, loyalty, and dissent. The policy becomes theater for domestic audiences rather than strategy for international stability.

That shift has consequences.

It pressures allies who require nuance. It radicalizes domestic discourse. It makes humanitarian law sound like weakness. It turns diplomacy into an identity contest.

Trump's vibe is not neutral. It is partial.

And partiality, when projected by a superpower, becomes destabilizing.

Allies do not merely want the United States to be powerful. They want it to be predictable. They want it to be disciplined enough that their own stability does not depend on one man's temperament.

Foreign policy by vibe makes temperament central.

It also makes flattery disproportionately influential.

Leaders who praise Trump publicly receive a warmer posture than leaders who criticize him, regardless of policy alignment. This creates a perverse incentive structure. Foreign leaders learn that the path to American goodwill is not necessarily through strategic partnership, but through performative admiration.

Diplomacy becomes a personality management exercise.

This is exhausting for allies and advantageous for adversaries.

Adversaries are often more willing to flatter if it buys confusion or delay. They can offer compliments cheaply. They can praise Trump's "strength" while testing American resolve. The flattery is a tool, not a belief.

Foreign policy by vibe is vulnerable to manipulation because it rewards emotional inputs.

It is also hostile to institutions.

Traditional foreign policy is mediated by agencies, diplomats, analysts, and legal frameworks. It depends on the process. Trump's vibe treats the process as an obstruction. When experts introduce nuance, they are dismissed as "globalists," "bureaucrats," or "weak." When diplomats caution about consequences, they are framed as undermining strength.

Strength, in this worldview, is not the ability to manage complexity.

It is the ability to ignore it.

This is why foreign policy becomes improvisational.

Not in the sense that nothing is planned, but in the sense that decisions are often shaped by momentary posture rather than coherent strategy. The improvisation looks decisive on television. It can even produce short-term wins.

But it creates long-term instability.

Allies begin to doubt.

Adversaries begin to probe.

Neutral actors begin to hedge.

The system responds by reducing risk-taking. Coordination becomes slower. Intelligence sharing becomes cautious. Consensus-building becomes harder.

All of this is invisible to domestic audiences until crisis reveals it.

Foreign policy by vibe also domesticates global conflict in another way: it treats international institutions as legitimacy machines that must be owned, not as frameworks that must be preserved.

Trump's skepticism toward alliances and multilateral bodies—NATO, the United Nations, international courts—is not purely ideological. It is emotional. These bodies require shared constraint. They dilute individual dominance. They insist on rules that apply even to the powerful.

Trump dislikes that posture.

The vibe prefers unilateral control because control feels like strength. Shared constraint feels like weakness, even when it protects American interests by distributing the burden and building legitimacy.

This preference weakens the architecture that the United States benefits from.

It also invites a strategic contradiction: Trump wants to be seen as the strongest leader on the world stage, but he undermines the very systems that amplify American power. American power abroad is not just military. It is alliance-based. It is institutional. It is reputational. It depends on trust that the United States will show up consistently.

Vibe undermines consistency.

The strongest foreign policies are boring because they are reliable. They do not require constant performance because they are supported by stable institutions. Trump's foreign policy requires constant performance because the performance is the policy.

That requirement creates volatility at home as well.

Domestic audiences are trained to view foreign conflicts through personality and loyalty rather than interest and law. Nuance is treated as suspect. Human rights language is dismissed as weakness. Diplomacy is framed as submission unless it produces a dramatic televised "win."

This framing is corrosive.

It reduces the public's capacity to understand tradeoffs. It increases polarization. It turns foreign policy into a permanent identity contest. It makes thoughtful disagreement difficult because thoughtful disagreement looks like disloyalty.

Part III of this book tracks the sequel's evolution: the rerun normalizes abnormality, acceleration outruns oversight, loyalty filters dissent, and crisis becomes atmosphere.

Foreign policy by vibe is the international expression of that same method.

It treats the world as a stage and power as a feeling. It privileges strongman aesthetics. It discounts vulnerability. It rewards flattery. It punishes nuance.

And because it is mood-driven, it is hard to anchor.

Allies cannot plan around mood.

Adversaries can exploit it.

Institutions cannot stabilize it.

The cost is not always immediate.

But it is cumulative.

Credibility leaks. Deterrence softens. Trust thins. The architecture of stability begins to creak.

Foreign policy by vibe does not always produce catastrophes in one dramatic moment.

It produces a world that is less certain that the United States means what it says.

And in international affairs, uncertainty is rarely neutral.

It is an invitation.

CHAPTER 18: LAW AND ORDER AS SPECTACLE

The sequel does not abandon law and order.

It repurposes it.

Donald Trump does not treat law and order as a system designed to protect the public evenly. He treats it as a visual language—a way to signal dominance, loyalty, and control. Enforcement becomes symbolic. Punishment becomes performative. Justice becomes something to be seen, not something to be measured.

Law and order becomes spectacle.

In traditional governance, enforcement is meant to be boring. It is procedural, constrained, and often invisible. Its legitimacy comes from consistency and restraint. Trump rejects that model. He governs through contrast. The louder the display, the stronger the message.

Visibility becomes power.

Trump's rhetoric around crime and punishment emphasizes fear over data. Isolated incidents are elevated into narratives of collapse. Cities are framed as lawless. Protest becomes threat. Disorder is exaggerated to justify response.

The spectacle requires an audience.

Trump's law-and-order posture is not primarily about reducing crime. It is about demonstrating authority. Images of force—officers in riot gear, federal agents deployed, crowds dispersed—become proof of leadership. Whether these actions improve safety is secondary.

What matters is how they look.

This approach reshapes priorities. Resources flow toward visible enforcement rather than preventive infrastructure. Crackdowns are favored over reform. Punitive responses are framed as decisive while structural solutions are dismissed as weak.

The sequel intensifies this logic.

Trump no longer needs to persuade the public that disorder exists. The narrative is already familiar. Crime is presented as omnipresent. Danger is assumed. The response is framed as overdue.

Fear becomes currency.

Fear compresses debate. When danger feels immediate, questions about proportionality sound indulgent. When threats feel constant, restraint looks irresponsible.

Trump exploits this compression.

He frames enforcement as moral clarity. Those targeted are not merely suspects; they are enemies. Dissenters are not citizens exercising rights; they are agitators undermining order.

This framing collapses complexity.

It blurs distinctions between protest and crime, between disorder and dissent, between enforcement and suppression. The law becomes a tool of categorization: loyal or disloyal, protected or punishable.

Law enforcement is pulled into politics.

Officers are praised when they align with Trump's narrative and criticized when they do not. Federal agencies are evaluated by responsiveness to political demand rather than adherence to standards. Neutrality becomes suspect.

The badge becomes symbolic.

Trump's posture also alters expectations around punishment. Severity is celebrated. Mercy is treated as weakness. Due process is reframed as delay. Accountability is dismissed as an obstruction.

Speed becomes virtue.

This emphasis on speed mirrors other aspects of the sequel. Enforcement actions are announced quickly, often with limited explanation. The spectacle precedes justification. By the time scrutiny arrives, the moment has passed.

Oversight struggles to keep up.

The spectacle also functions as a distraction. Highly visible enforcement absorbs attention that might otherwise focus on policy failures or structural issues. The drama of crackdowns crowds out quieter questions about efficacy.

Trump benefits from this shift.

He positions himself as the embodiment of order amid the chaos he describes. The presence of disorder becomes evidence of the need for his authority. Resolution is less important than continuation.

Law and order must never fully succeed.

If crime were truly solved, the spectacle would end. The narrative requires an ongoing threat to justify ongoing force.

This creates a paradox.

The stated goal is safety. The operational goal is dominance. When dominance requires disorder to justify itself, safety becomes secondary.

The sequel reveals this tension.

Trump's rhetoric celebrates enforcement but resists accountability. When enforcement fails to reduce crime or creates harm, blame is redirected. Critics are accused of sympathizing with criminals. Structural factors are ignored.

This deflection protects the spectacle.

Law enforcement officers themselves are caught in the middle. They are elevated rhetorically but constrained operationally. Expectations rise while support fluctuates. Political loyalty is emphasized over institutional independence.

The result is strain.

Departments face pressure to perform toughness without the resources or policy backing to address underlying causes. Morale fluctuates. Trust erodes.

Spectacle undermines legitimacy.

When enforcement is perceived as political theater, public cooperation declines. Communities withdraw. Information dries up. Safety becomes harder to achieve.

Trump's law-and-order spectacle also intersects with race.

The imagery of disorder is racialized. Certain communities are portrayed as inherently threatening. Enforcement appears uneven. Disparities are dismissed as coincidence.

This framing deepens division.

Law becomes conditional.

Loyalty determines who is protected and who is targeted. Criticism invites scrutiny. Alignment invites leniency.

This personalization erodes the rule of law.

The rule of law depends on predictability and impartiality. Spectacle thrives on surprise and discretion.

Trump chooses spectacle.

This chapter does not argue that enforcement is unnecessary. Public safety matters. Order matters. But when law and order become a stage rather than a system, their meaning shifts.

Justice becomes something to perform, not something to uphold.

The sequel's law-and-order posture reflects the broader pattern of Part II.

Law and order as spectacle feels strong.

But it weakens institutions.

The danger is erosion disguised as strength.

PART IV

CHAPTER 19: THE LAW BENDS SOUTH

The sequel produces consequences.

They do not fall evenly.

Donald Trump does not change the law everywhere at once. He bends it. And the bend has direction. It moves south—toward borders, detention centers, court dockets crowded with migrants, and communities already conditioned to expect the harshest reading of authority.

The law does not break.

It angles.

This angling matters. Laws that remain formally intact can still be applied selectively. Rights that exist on paper can thin in practice. Due process can be slowed, narrowed, or rendered unreachable without ever being abolished. The appearance of legality remains even as access to it recedes.

The consequence is not a single policy.

It is a pattern.

Trump's approach to immigration enforcement treats the border not as a legal threshold, but as a proving ground for executive will. The farther one is from political power, the more flexible the law becomes. Discretion expands downward, away from scrutiny and toward populations with the least capacity to resist.

This is not new in American history.

But it is intensified.

In the sequel, enforcement is framed as necessity rather than choice. Migration is described as invasion. Asylum is recast as fraud. Human movement becomes threat. Once framed this way, restraint looks reckless and care looks naïve.

Urgency licenses exception.

The border becomes a space where norms are suspended without being named as such. Procedures compress. Timelines shorten. Access to counsel narrows. The promise of individualized review fades behind mass processing and administrative throughput.

The law bends without announcing itself.

Trump's rhetoric does not emphasize legality. It emphasizes volume. Numbers replace nuance. The problem is not individual cases, but scale. When scale becomes the enemy, process becomes expendable.

Efficiency is elevated above fairness.

Families are separated through administrative momentum rather than explicit design. Detention expands through contractual logic rather than legislative debate. Deportation accelerates through procedural shortcuts rather than judicial review.

No single actor owns the harm.

The system does.

Trump's defenders frame this as deterrence. Harshness, they argue, discourages future crossings. Suffering becomes strategy. The law is bent to teach a lesson rather than deliver justice.

But deterrence does not require legality to weaken.

Only empathy.

This is where the bend deepens.

The farther south enforcement travels, the less visible its effects become to the broader public. Detention centers operate away from cameras. Hearings occur in remote jurisdictions. Outcomes are buried in statistics rather than stories.

Distance dilutes scrutiny.

Distance also racializes consequences. The populations most affected are disproportionately people of color. The law's flexibility tracks vulnerability. Enforcement feels absolute to those with the least capacity to contest it.

Equality thins at the margins.

Trump's approach does not openly reject due process. It reframes it as indulgence. Hearings are delayed. Appeals are loopholes. Legal advocacy is obstruction.

Process becomes suspect.

This framing seeps into the courts. Caseloads balloon. Timelines compress. Judges face pressure to move cases quickly. Individual narratives blur into categories.

Justice becomes administrative.

The bend south is not limited to immigration courts. It extends to the broader conception of who is entitled to protection. Noncitizens are framed as guests rather than rights-bearing individuals. Their claims are evaluated through suspicion rather than presumption.

Suspicion replaces neutrality.

Trump's public language reinforces this hierarchy. Citizenship becomes a moral credential. Those without it are described as drains, criminals, or invaders. The line between legal status and moral worth blurs.

The law bends toward exclusion.

This exclusion is normalized through repetition. Policies are announced, challenged, partially revised, then reintroduced. Each iteration pushes the boundary slightly further. Fatigue replaces outrage.

Incrementalism masks impact.

By the time courts intervene, damage is already dispersed. Families are separated. Lives are disrupted. Time is lost. Remedies cannot fully restore what enforcement has already taken.

The law may correct itself eventually.

The harm does not wait.

Trump's approach also relies on jurisdictional complexity. Federal authority overlaps with state cooperation. Local enforcement is incentivized. Accountability fragments.

Responsibility diffuses.

When harm occurs, blame travels downward. Officers followed policy. Agencies followed directives. Directives followed necessity. Necessity followed crisis.

The chain dissolves.

This is the architecture of bending rather than breaking. No single rule is abolished. No rights are explicitly revoked. The system shifts until the outcome changes.

The bend south also intersects with geopolitics. Asylum claims tied to violence abroad are treated skeptically even as U.S. foreign policy contributes to instability. Responsibility is displaced outward.

Cause and effect separate.

The law's posture becomes defensive rather than protective. Its primary function shifts from safeguarding rights to managing flow. Human beings become variables in a logistical equation.

This instrumentalization has consequences beyond immigration.

It trains institutions to treat legality as flexible when dealing with marginalized populations. It conditions officials to see discretion as a tool rather than responsibility. It normalizes exception as baseline.

The bend travels.

Part IV begins here because consequence is not abstract. It is geographic. It lands in specific places, on specific people, through mechanisms that are easy to ignore from a distance.

The sequel does not announce cruelty.

It administers it.

Trump's defenders argue that sovereignty requires firmness. Borders matter. Laws must be enforced. These claims are not false. But enforcement without proportionality is not firmness.

It is a distortion.

The law bends south, not because it must.

But because it can.

Power tests its reach where resistance is weakest. It experiments at the margins before moving inward. What happens at the border rarely stays there.

Precedent migrates.

If due process can be compromised here, it can be compromised elsewhere. If discretion can override rights in this case, it can do so again. The bend becomes a template.

This chapter does not claim inevitability.

It traces a trajectory.

Consequences accumulate when systems reward speed over care, volume over judgment, and spectacle over restraint. The border is the first place this logic lands because it is politically convenient and morally distant.

But distance does not make it separate.

Part IV examines what happens when methods finally settle into outcomes—when acceleration, loyalty, crisis, vibe, and spectacle converge on people with the least power to resist.

The law bends south.

The question is how far it bends before it breaks.

CHAPTER 20: ARSONIST AS FIREFIGHTER

The sequel does not merely create problems.

It stages their rescue.

Donald Trump governs by ignition. He introduces disruption, escalates it, and then re-enters the scene, presenting himself as the only figure capable of restoring order. The fire is not accidental. It is functional. The damage is not collateral. It is a narrative setup.

Trump is not responding to the crisis.

He is manufacturing it.

This pattern repeats across domains. Policy is introduced abruptly, without preparation or mitigation. Predictable harm follows. The harm is amplified rhetorically. And then the same authority that caused the damage offers relief—framed as generosity, strength, or decisive leadership.

The firefighter arrives with cameras already rolling.

The genius of this approach lies in timing. The rescue does not come too early, when responsibility might still be obvious. It comes after confusion sets in, after stakeholders scramble, after blame disperses. By the time the fix is offered, the origin of the fire has faded.

Memory is short.

Damage is loud.

Trump relies on this asymmetry.

The pattern is clearest in economic policy, particularly tariffs. Trump raises tariffs broadly—against adversaries and allies alike—framing the move as toughness. The consequences arrive quickly and predictably. Supply chains tighten. Prices rise. Farmers lose markets. Retaliation follows.

The fire spreads.

Rather than acknowledge causation, Trump reframes impact as evidence of sacrifice. Pain becomes patriotism. Loss becomes proof of resolve. The policy is defended not by outcome, but by posture.

Then comes the rescue.

Subsidies are proposed. Grants are announced. Relief packages are framed as a benevolent intervention. Trump positions himself as a savior to the very constituencies his policy has destabilized.

The firefighter stands in the smoke.

The contradiction is normalized. Trump does not deny causing the harm. He reframes it as necessary destruction. Relief is presented not as correction, but as reward.

This reframing shifts accountability.

The audience is encouraged to thank the rescuer rather than question the arsonist. Gratitude replaces scrutiny. Dependency replaces evaluation.

This dynamic repeats beyond tariffs.

Regulatory rollbacks create instability. Enforcement crackdowns generate backlash. Abrupt policy reversals produce uncertainty. Each time, Trump steps in to "fix" the chaos—often temporarily, often selectively, often with conditions.

Relief is contingent.

Control deepens.

The arsonist-firefighter pattern thrives on selective empathy. Relief is extended where loyalty exists. Aid is withheld where dissent persists. The rescue becomes a loyalty test.

Governance becomes conditional.

Trump's approach to disaster response reflects the same logic. Crises are framed as failures of others until Trump intervenes. Aid is delayed, accelerated, or politicized. Praise is rewarded. Criticism is punished.

The fire determines leverage.

This approach reframes competence. Traditional governance aims to prevent harm. Trump's model aims to dominate recovery. Prevention is invisible. Rescue is theatrical.

The spectacle matters more than the outcome.

The arsonist-firefighter pattern blurs causality. By collapsing problem and solution into the same figure, Trump creates a closed loop of authority.

There is no external benchmark.

There is no alternative.

The public is presented with a false binary: accept damage and rescue, or face chaos without intervention.

This is design.

Trump's defenders call this deal-making. But governance is not negotiation theater. When pressure is inflicted on the public, concessions come at real cost.

The cost is borne unevenly.

Farmers lose income. Workers face uncertainty. Consumers absorb price increases. Relief arrives late, selectively, and often insufficiently.

The fire leaves residue.

Institutions weaken. Agencies react rather than plan. Preparedness gives way to improvisation. Strategy collapses under short-term fixes.

The system becomes brittle.

Trump thrives in this environment.

The arsonist-firefighter model relies on repetition. Each cycle dulls awareness. Chaos normalizes. Expectations lower.

Accountability erodes.

Trump occupies both sides of the narrative: destroyer and savior. Criticism of the fire becomes ingratitude toward the firefighter.

The trap closes.

This chapter is not about incompetence.

It is about method.

The arsonist-firefighter model scales poorly. Small fires can be managed theatrically. Large ones cannot.

Eventually, the firefighter arrives too late.

Part IV traces accumulation. Each rescue weakens the structure it claims to save.

The fire is never extinguished.

It is curated.

Trump does not govern to solve problems.

He governs the problems.

CHAPTER 21: PEACE, LOUDLY

Peace is claimed often here. Peace, in the sequel, is not quiet.
It is announced.

Donald Trump does not present peace as a condition to be maintained. He presents it as a personal achievement to be claimed. Peace becomes a headline, a tally, a brand. It is measured not by durability, verification, or institutional consensus, but by declaration.

Peace is spoken into existence.

Trump repeatedly claims to have solved, ended, or stabilized foreign conflicts—often without timelines, third-party confirmation, or durable agreements. The announcement arrives first. The verification, if it arrives at all, comes later. Sometimes it never comes.

The performance precedes the proof.

In traditional diplomacy, peace is recognized after it is achieved. Agreements are signed. Ceasefires are monitored. Compliance is measured. Trump reverses this sequence. He declares success and treats follow-through as optional.

The declaration becomes the achievement.

Trump frames himself as a singular peacemaker—someone uniquely capable of resolving conflicts others failed to address. Institutions are sidelined. Alliances are minimized. Process is dismissed as unnecessary when instinct is elevated.

Credit is centralized.

This centralization feeds a visible ambition: international validation. Trump repeatedly signals that his actions merit recognition at the highest level, including the Nobel Peace Prize. The prize becomes shorthand for legitimacy.

Recognition becomes the goal.

The problem is not aspiration. It is a contradiction.

Trump's peace narrative exists alongside behavior that escalates tension, destabilizes regions, and heightens risk. Threats are issued publicly. Military force is discussed casually. Escalation is framed as leverage rather than a last resort.

Peace is claimed with one hand.

Pressure is applied with the other.

This contradiction weakens credibility.

Allies hesitate to endorse claims that lack verification. Adversaries discount declarations that are not anchored to restraint. Neutral observers treat peace announcements as rhetorical positioning rather than operational reality.

Peace becomes noise.

Trump's definition of resolution also shifts meaning. Reduced visibility becomes success. Delay becomes victory. Silence becomes peace.

Unresolved does not mean concluded.

It means unexamined.

Conflicts that continue without formal settlement are nonetheless counted as solved in rhetoric. The absence of immediate headlines is treated as an achievement.

This convenience is unstable.

The peace narrative also collapses when placed alongside Trump's actions elsewhere. While claiming to stabilize foreign regions, he introduces instability in others. He praises strongmen in one breath and threatens adversaries in the next.

Consistency dissolves.

The contradiction is even sharper when peace claims are contrasted with domestic posture. While branding himself a global peacemaker, Trump governs domestically through fear, emergency language, and forceful imagery.

Peace is externalized.

Control is internalized.

Military language enters domestic politics. Disorder is exaggerated. Crisis is sustained. Calm is delayed. Stability is conditional.

Peace abroad becomes difficult to defend when fear is weaponized at home.

Trump's defenders argue that strength prevents war. That unpredictability deters conflict. That public threats keep adversaries cautious. These arguments are not new.

But deterrence depends on restraint.

Unpredictability without restraint is volatility.

Trump's rhetoric often blurs deterrence and provocation. Casual threats raise stakes. Public escalation invites response. The margin for miscalculation narrows.

Peace becomes precarious.

The Nobel Peace Prize aspiration highlights the gap between branding and practice. Historically, the prize recognizes sustained efforts toward reconciliation, institution-building, and verifiable agreements.

Trump emphasizes announcement over architecture.

Architecture is slow.

Announcement is fast.

Peace requires tending.

Trump prefers declaring.

Agreements require maintenance. Ceasefires require monitoring. Trust requires consistency. Trump's approach prioritizes credit at the moment of announcement, not responsibility over time.

Peace becomes possession rather than obligation.

This personalization makes peace fragile. When peace is tied to one individual, it dissolves when attention shifts. Stability becomes dependent on temperament rather than structure.

Temperament does not endure.

The louder the peace claim, the greater the scrutiny. Trump treats scrutiny as hostility. Verification is framed as doubt. Doubt becomes disloyalty.

Correction shuts down.

Peace without correction decays.

This chapter does not deny Trump's desire to be seen as a peacemaker. It examines how the pursuit of recognition distorts the work of peacemaking. When peace becomes a trophy, the labor that sustains it becomes secondary.

Noise replaces signal.

Part IV traces consequence as accumulation. Chapter 21 marks the moment where contradiction can no longer be smoothed over. Peace is declared while instability persists. Recognition is sought while credibility thins.

The distance between claim and condition widens.

Peace, loudly proclaimed, convinces fewer people each time.

The question is not whether peace is possible.

It is whether peace can survive when treated as branding rather than an obligation.

CHAPTER 22: CLEAN HANDS, FULL POCKETS

Efficiency is one of the safest words in Donald Trump sells reform the way a casino sells "free drinks."

It's loud, fast, generously advertised—and, if you're paying attention, it's never actually free. There is always a cost. The only question is who pays it and when.

In Part IV we arrive at consequence, the stage where the method stops feeling like rhetoric and starts feeling like missing services, hollowed departments, and people who did nothing wrong discovering that "efficiency" is just another word for being erased on a spreadsheet. This is where Trump's sequel becomes less about performance and more about damage management: who gets protected, who gets sacrificed, and who gets to call it progress.

Enter DOGE.

The branding alone is a confession. It's a wink disguised as policy: a name that sounds like a meme, a mascot for swaggering disruption, the kind of thing you put on a hoodie before you gut a program that keeps someone alive. DOGE is presented as a crusade against "waste," "fraud," and "corruption"—three words that, in Trump's world, function like incense. They smell righteous. They make audiences feel clean. They also distract from the details that would reveal who is actually benefiting from the cleansing.

DOGE arrives with a promise: it will find the rot, cut it out, and deliver a leaner, stronger government.

The promise is emotionally satisfying because it is simple. Everyone hates waste. Everyone resents corruption. Everyone can imagine a bloated office somewhere doing nothing while real people struggle. The fantasy is that a fearless outsider will walk in, flip the lights on, and expose the scam.

But DOGE is not built on exposure.

It is built on authority—authority to decide what counts as waste, what counts as corruption, and which cuts are "necessary" because urgency is always the excuse.

The leadership choice makes the contradiction impossible to ignore, even if the administration expects you to ignore it.

Trump selects an ultra-wealthy private-sector figure—someone whose wealth is not merely personal but structural, built in part through entanglement with government contracts, public subsidies, regulatory ecosystems, and the kind of state cooperation that no billionaire likes to admit they depend on. The choice is sold as brilliance: "Who better to eliminate corruption than someone too rich to be bought?"

It's a clever line.

It's also an escape hatch. Because "too rich to be bought" is not the same thing as "unconflicted." A person can be beyond bribery and still be drenched in incentives. A person can be wealthy enough to ignore petty influence and still be deeply motivated by power, expansion, and the perpetual growth that turns a fortune into a kingdom.

DOGE is framed as a disinfectant. In practice, it becomes a solvent—dissolving oversight, dissolving institutional memory, dissolving the simple guardrails that prevent a government from becoming a private playground for the powerful.

Here is the mechanics of it.

First, DOGE announces targets the way Trump announces enemies: with confidence, contempt, and an undertone of "how dare anyone question this." Agencies are described not as complex systems that deliver services, but as "bureaucracies" that exist to slow "real Americans" down. Programs are reduced to slogans. Entire departments are flattened into accusations.

Then comes the purge of the public narrative.

DOGE does not begin with proof. It begins with a premise: corruption is everywhere, and urgency is the reason evidence is optional. The public is invited to applaud cuts as moral victories rather than examine them as choices. The language of triage is used to avoid the language of consequence.

And consequences arrive quickly.

Agencies that provide lifesaving services abroad are closed or defunded on the grounds that the United States should stop "paying for the world." This sells well in soundbites because generosity can be reframed as weakness. But these programs are not charity. They are strategy. They prevent disease spread. They stabilize regions. They build relationships that matter when crises hit. They create goodwill that cannot be purchased at the last minute with a press conference.

When those programs vanish, the suffering is not abstract.

Clinics stop operating. Vaccination campaigns stall. Food assistance is interrupted. Local partners collapse under the weight of promises that evaporate. The costs show up later—in refugees, in instability, in emergency spending that dwarfs the original budget.

DOGE calls this "savings."

It is deferred expense.

At home, DOGE aims at the federal workforce like it is a bloated organism rather than a network of people who run safety inspections, monitor public health, protect infrastructure, investigate fraud, manage disasters, and keep the basic machinery of the country functioning. Workers are fired in batches, framed as "cuts to bureaucracy," as if bureaucracy were a species rather than a set of tasks that someone still has to do.

The consequences are immediate in the places that rely on quiet competence.

Backlogs grow. Oversight thins. Response times lengthen. Mistakes increase because experienced staff are replaced by vacancies. DOGE claims efficiency while eliminating the very capacity that makes efficiency possible. It's like bragging about making a ship lighter by throwing overboard the crew.

All of this might still be debated as ideology—small government versus big—if DOGE were simply a policy preference.

But DOGE is not only about size.

It is about who gets to define corruption while living inside it.

The conflict of interest is not a side detail; it is the central betrayal. DOGE's leadership maintains or benefits from enormous government contracts and public resources—contracts that create leverage, dependencies, and opportunities. The administration insists this is irrelevant because the leader is "a genius" and "results-oriented," and because Trump's vocabulary has one powerful disinfectant word for everything: "success."

Success is the shield.

If money is flowing to the right people, it must be success. If a contract expands, it must be innovation. If oversight is reduced, it must be efficiency. DOGE's mission becomes inverted: instead of eliminating corruption, it eliminates the definitions that could label it as such.

This is where the evidence problem becomes moral.

DOGE makes sweeping claims—about waste uncovered, fraud eliminated, savings achieved—without providing transparent, verifiable substantiation at the level the public deserves. Audits are replaced by assertions. Metrics are selectively presented. Criticism is framed as defense of corruption.

The trap is perfect.

If you demand evidence, you are accused of protecting waste. If you question the motives, you are accused of "hating success." If you ask who benefits, you are accused of being jealous or ideological. The public is pushed into a binary: cheer the cuts or be labeled part of the problem.

This is not reform.

This is narrative discipline.

And narrative discipline is how Trump governs.

DOGE also reveals something about Trump's relationship to the word "corruption."

Corruption, in the Trump worldview, is not an objective category. It is a weapon. It describes people who resist him and absolves people who serve him. It is shouted at opponents and ignored in allies. It is performed rather than enforced.

So DOGE becomes a stage where Trump can attack institutions that constrain him while empowering individuals whose private incentives align with his needs.

That is the function of selective austerity.

DOGE is not a neutral scalpel; it is a directional knife.

It cuts programs that help the vulnerable first because those programs are politically easy to caricature. It cuts agencies that regulate powerful industries because those cuts benefit donors, allies, and the broader ideology of deregulation. It cuts workers whose jobs are invisible to television, because invisible labor is easy to dismiss.

Then DOGE leaves untouched—or actively expands—the parts of government that feed the private empires connected to its leadership. Contracts remain. Deals flourish. "Public-private partnerships" become the new language of expansion. Government is downsized where it serves people and enlarged where it serves profit.

DOGE calls this modernization.

It is privatization with better lighting.

The cost is trust.

A government can cut programs and still retain legitimacy if the cuts are transparent, evidence-based, and fairly distributed. DOGE does not offer that fairness. It offers a vibe: "We're cleaning house." But the house being cleaned is always the room where poor people live, while the penthouse remains untouched and somehow keeps collecting rent.

This is where the anti-corruption pose becomes grotesque.

Because the result is not a cleaner government.

It is a less accountable one.

DOGE undermines the very mechanisms that detect corruption—inspectors general, watchdog offices, compliance systems—by framing them as bureaucratic waste. The system's immune response is treated as disease.

Once the immune system is weakened, infection spreads.

And because DOGE is branded as reform, the public is encouraged to interpret the damage as necessary pain rather than as the predictable consequence of dismantling guardrails.

Trump loves this logic.

It allows him to claim moral superiority while delivering material advantage to aligned interests. It allows him to frame critics as defenders of waste while the real waste—massive, structural, often contractual—continues unchallenged.

The most cynical aspect is that DOGE's harms are sold as patriotism.

People are told that losing services is sacrifice, that losing stability is toughness, that losing safeguards is freedom. But freedom without protections is not freedom. It is exposure. It is the freedom of the powerful to expand and the freedom of everyone else to suffer quietly.

The chapter ends where it must: with the recognition that "anti-corruption" in the Trump sequel is less a program than a posture. DOGE is a shiny tool built to cut the parts of government that serve the public while leaving untouched the parts that serve private power.

The hands are called clean.

The pockets are still full.

And the evidence—like so much else in this era—is treated as optional.

CHAPTER 23: CARVING THE NAME INTO HISTORY

Donald Trump's relationship with history is not respectful.

It is possessive.

He does not look at the past as something to learn from. He looks at it as something to be edited—something to be rebranded so that it flatters him, protects him, and, most importantly, keeps him central. This is not merely ego. It is strategy. If you can control the story a nation tells about itself, you can control what the nation tolerates.

Trump understands a simple truth: names last.

A policy can be repealed. A memo can be forgotten. A scandal can be blurred by time. But a name carved in stone becomes a kind of national muscle memory. People repeat it without thinking. Tourists photograph it. Children memorize it. History becomes a hallway lined with plaques, and the plaques teach the public who mattered.

Trump wants plaques.

He wants the aesthetics of inevitability—the kind of permanence that makes future arguments feel pointless because "look, it's already on the building." That is why he flirts with the idea of putting himself on Mount Rushmore, why he entertains naming naval fleets after him, why he fixates on attaching his name to institutions like the Kennedy Center, why he pushes for naming government buildings in a way that treats the public sector like a branding opportunity.

This is not a new human instinct.

It is a very old one.

It is the instinct of rulers.

Democratic leaders tend to leave legacy through institutions: laws, norms, systems that outlive them. Autocratic leaders tend to leave legacy through symbols: statues, portraits, names on monuments. Symbols demand less accountability. A statue does not have to work. A name does not have to pass an audit.

It only has to stand.

Trump's obsession with naming is the domestic version of foreign policy by vibe. It is legacy by aesthetic. It replaces substance with spectacle and calls the spectacle "history."

The impulse becomes even clearer when Trump turns to museums and memory.

Museums are dangerous in the Trump worldview because they preserve complexity. They insist on context. They require the nation to confront parts of itself that do not feel flattering. They show the cost of national success, not only the triumph.

Trump does not like cost.

He prefers victory narratives—clean, heroic, simple. That is why he pressures cultural institutions to "soften" the story of slavery, to eliminate references that make the nation feel guilty, to present the past as a clean upward march rather than a complicated struggle built on contradictions.

This is not about education.

It is about comfort.

And comfort, politically, is a form of control.

When a society is taught to avoid discomfort, it becomes easier to manipulate. The public becomes allergic to truth that requires responsibility. People learn to interpret critique as an attack and history as an insult. That is how you create a population that can be governed through grievance rather than through reality.

Trump weaponizes that grievance.

He frames honest accounts of slavery not as factual correction, but as "hate" for America. He frames educators and curators not as stewards of knowledge, but as ideological enemies. The public is taught that confronting injustice is weakness and that erasing discomfort is patriotism.

Patriotism becomes denial in a flag costume.

The monument obsession is not separate from this museum obsession. They are part of one project: to redesign national memory so that Trump's preferred story becomes the default.

The story is simple:

America is perfect.

Critics are traitors.

Trump is the defender of greatness.

History must flatter the present.

To accomplish this, Trump does not need to convince historians.
He needs to intimidate institutions.
Naming becomes leverage.

When a leader flirts publicly with putting his name on iconic spaces, he signals to every institution that legacy is political property. He shifts the question from "What does this place represent?" to "Who has power to define what it represents?"

The Kennedy Center, for example, is not merely a building. It is a symbol of cultural legitimacy. Attaching a name to it is attaching a narrative to it. The same is true for federal buildings, museums, parks, and historic sites. Names are moral claims.

Trump wants the claim without the accountability.

That is why he treats public spaces like real estate. He assumes naming rights are a natural reward for power. If you are the president, why shouldn't the country look like you? Why shouldn't the buildings behave like billboards?

Because the public is not private property.

But Trump's brand-oriented worldview struggles to grasp that distinction. His instinct is that everything is negotiable, purchasable, and renamable. He behaves as though the nation is a portfolio, and legacy is the logo you stamp on it.

This creates a second danger: when naming becomes a political reward, history becomes partisan loot.

Monuments become trophies.

Museums become battlegrounds.

Archives become targets.

And once you have introduced the idea that the past can be edited to protect feelings, the future becomes more fragile. Because if a society cannot tell the truth about its past, it becomes less capable of telling the truth about its present.

Trump's legacy project is also a distraction.

A president obsessed with carving his name into stone is often a president avoiding accountability for what he does in office. The monument becomes a substitute for accomplishment. It is the "certificate of greatness" you print yourself when history refuses to issue one.

The desire to rename battleship fleets after him fits the same psychology. Ships are symbols of strength. They are steel mythology. A ship named after a leader is a floating monument, a moving billboard that travels the world with the name attached.

Trump wants that.

He wants his power to have a logo.

But what does it mean when a leader obsessed with branding also wants museums to soften slavery's story? It means the project is not only self-glorification. It is a narrative defense. If the nation confronts slavery honestly, it confronts ongoing inequality honestly. If it confronts inequality honestly, it may demand policy changes. If it demands changes, it may threaten the power structures that sustain Trump's coalition.

So history must be edited.

Not because the past changes, but because the present is threatened by the truth.

This is why the phrase "eliminate references to slavery" is not just cultural politics. It is governance by amnesia. It is the attempt to sever cause from consequence. If slavery is softened, its legacy becomes easier to dismiss. If the legacy is dismissed, then modern disparities can be framed as personal failure rather than systemic residue.

That is how you protect hierarchy.

Trump's monument obsession is, in this sense, a continuation of Chapter 19's "bend." The law bends at the margins. History bends in the museums. Both bends move in the same direction: toward comfort for the powerful and away from accountability for harm.

The public is asked to accept this bending as patriotism.

But patriotism that requires editing reality is not patriotism.

It is insecurity.

A mature nation can hold complexity. It can honor its achievements while acknowledging its crimes. It can tell the truth without collapsing. That maturity is the foundation of resilience.

Trump offers a different model:

Erase discomfort.

Brand greatness.

Carve the name.

Call it history.

This chapter is not about whether Trump deserves a monument. It is about why he wants one so badly. Because a leader who demands permanence is often a leader who fears judgment. A name in stone is a preemptive argument with the future.

It says:

You will remember me this way, whether you like it or not.

But history is not a building you can rename.

It is a record you have to face.

And the more aggressively a leader tries to carve his name into the nation's icons, the louder he admits that the icons alone cannot prove his greatness.

He needs the stone to do what reality won't.

So he tries to make the nation a billboard.

And in doing so, he reveals the most fragile thing of all:
a leader who cannot tolerate a history that does not revolve around him.

Trump's naming obsession also exposes how he understands legitimacy: not as something earned through service, but as something conferred through visibility. If your name is everywhere, you must matter. If your name is etched into the landscape, disagreement begins to feel like vandalism. This is why authoritarian-leaning politics loves monuments. Monuments are arguments you don't have to win again.

The same impulse shows up in smaller, quieter ways: in the insistence that official statements use preferred phrases, in the demand that agencies adopt flattering language, in the anger at historians who refuse to "balance" slavery with the convenience-store version of American virtue. Trump wants a country that speaks his adjectives.

And because he understands branding better than governance, he treats public memory like market share. If museums tell a more honest story, he feels personally diminished. If a monument does not include him, he feels excluded. This is not simply vanity—it is an attempt to discipline the nation's sense of self so that criticism of Trump becomes criticism of America.

That is the ultimate merger he seeks: to fuse his identity with the nation's. If "America" and "Trump" become interchangeable in public memory, then opposition becomes sacrilege. That fusion is why he fights so hard over curricula, exhibits, and plaques. He is not debating history; he is claiming ownership.

But history is stubborn. It leaks through edits. It survives soft language. It resurfaces through archives and testimony and the simple fact that people remember what happened to them, even when leaders try to rename the event.

So, the monument project never ends. It must be constantly maintained, constantly defended, constantly refreshed—because the truth keeps weathering the stone.

CHAPTER 24: JUSTICE, AIMED

The Department of Justice is supposed to be boring.

That is not an insult. That is the design. Its power is not in drama but in discipline, not in spectacle but in process. The DOJ is meant to be slow enough to be careful, independent enough to resist politics, and consistent enough that the public can trust that the law is not simply a weapon for whoever holds power.

Donald Trump hates boring.

He hates the distance. He hates the "no." He hates the idea that some parts of government are not built to serve his moods. He treats independence not as protection for democracy, but as betrayal of leadership.

So in the sequel, Trump attempts what he always attempts: to turn an institution into an extension of himself.

This is not always done through explicit orders. It is done through pressure, narrative, and staffing. The method mirrors what we have already seen: loyalty as qualification, crisis as atmosphere, spectacle as legitimacy.

The DOJ becomes a target because it is one of the few institutions capable of constraining him.

If you can bend the DOJ, you can turn law into leverage.

Trump's public approach is direct. He names enemies. He labels people "criminal." He demands investigations. He frames the absence of prosecution as proof of corruption. He treats the DOJ not as a neutral arbiter but as a tool that has been "stolen" by opponents.

He implies the fix is simple:

put it back in his hands.

This is the rhetorical foundation of weaponization.

Because weaponization begins with the claim that the other side did it first. If you can persuade the public that justice has already been politicized, then politicizing it further can be sold as restoration rather than takeover.

Trump becomes an expert at this inversion.

He calls the DOJ corrupt while pressuring it to behave corruptly. He accuses prosecutors of bias while demanding prosecution of his perceived enemies. He frames independence as conspiracy and loyalty as reform.

The irony is not subtle.

It is the point.

Trump's critics often focus on whether his attempts succeed. Many of them fail procedurally. Courts intervene. Norms hold in pockets. Officials resist. Cases do not materialize. Accusations do not become indictments.

But focusing only on procedural success misses the deeper political success: the corrosion.

Because weaponization does not need to succeed to damage the system.

It only needs to be attempted loudly.

When a president repeatedly demands prosecutions, he teaches the public to interpret justice as personal revenge. He teaches supporters that the law should punish enemies. He teaches opponents that the law is vulnerable. He teaches institutions that neutrality will be attacked regardless.

Trust drains.

This is the slow catastrophe: the conversion of the rule of law into a loyalty contest.

The DOJ, like other institutions, is staffed by people. And people respond to incentives. When Trump suggests that the DOJ should prosecute enemies, he also suggests that those who refuse are disloyal. When loyalty becomes a career risk, self-censorship grows.

Officials choose caution.

Not because they are corrupt,

but because the environment is.

That is how institutions bend without breaking.

Trump's weaponization attempts also rely on spectacle. The demand for justice is performed publicly. Press conferences hint at investigations. Names are floated. Accusations are repeated.

The public is not offered evidence.

The public is offered certainty.

This certainty creates expectations that are difficult for legal institutions to satisfy, because legal institutions require proof, procedure, and time. When the DOJ cannot deliver instant revenge, Trump frames that as proof of corruption. The system is pressured either to violate its standards or be punished politically for maintaining them.

It is a trap.

The DOJ becomes guilty either way.

Trump's persistence matters here. Even when efforts fail, he continues. He cannot stop because stopping would concede that the institution does not belong to him. Persistence becomes an assertion of ownership: he keeps pulling at the DOJ like a man yanking on a locked door, insisting the lock is illegitimate.

The door is not illegitimate.

The lock is democracy.

Trump's supporters interpret this insistence as strength. They like the idea of a president who will "fight back." They are told they are victims of a weaponized system. The solution is to weaponize it harder in the other direction.

Revenge becomes justice.

Justice becomes vengeance.

This is a profound shift in civic culture.

In a healthy democracy, the public may disagree about laws, policies, or outcomes, but there is a baseline belief that law is not simply a club for punishing enemies. When that belief erodes, the system becomes unstable. Each election becomes existential because the winner can potentially turn law into revenge.

Trump's weaponization narrative makes every contest existential by design.

It also pressures judges, prosecutors, and investigators through public intimidation. When officials are named and attacked, they become targets of harassment. Threats escalate. Security becomes necessary. Some people leave the profession. Others stay quiet.

The system loses talent.

The system loses courage.

The system loses independence.

Even if no prosecutions occur, the institution is weakened.

Trump's claims also create a parallel justice system: the public court of loyalty.

In this court, evidence is not required. Accusation is enough. "Everybody knows" becomes proof. Rumor becomes record. Social media becomes indictment. Talk shows become trials.

The real DOJ must compete with the fake DOJ of narrative.

The fake DOJ is faster.

It is louder.

It is more emotionally satisfying.

And because it is more satisfying, it shapes expectations. People begin to demand that the real DOJ behave like the fake one: immediate, punitive, personal.

When it refuses, trust declines.

This is the core danger of weaponization: it transforms public understanding of justice into entertainment.

Justice becomes something you watch, cheer, and share—rather than something you participate in through civic responsibility.

The sequel deepens this transformation because Trump has learned which levers matter most. He intensifies loyalty tests. He increases rhetorical pressure. He frames independence as sabotage. He positions himself as the only legitimate interpreter of justice.

Legitimacy becomes personal.

This chapter's irony is that Trump's weaponization attempts are often unsuccessful "as of to date" in the narrow procedural sense—cases do not materialize the way he wants, institutions resist fully collapsing, and courts limit overreach. But Trump's persistence still accomplishes damage.

Because the goal is not only to prosecute enemies.

The goal is to make the public believe that prosecution is the proper use of power.

That belief is the seed of authoritarianism.

It is the conversion of government from a shared system into a personal instrument.

Trump keeps trying because trying keeps the system unstable. It keeps supporters angry and mobilized. It keeps opponents defensive. It keeps institutions under pressure. It keeps the nation in a posture of suspicion.

Permanent suspicion is fertile ground for control.

The chapter closes with the uncomfortable truth that weaponization is not only something Trump attempts. It is something the country begins to normalize by arguing over it endlessly without drawing a hard line.

If citizens accept that the DOJ should be used against enemies, then democracy becomes an arms race: each administration must weaponize more to avoid being weaponized by the next.

That is not law.

That is revenge with a letterhead.

The DOJ is designed to be boring so it can be trusted.

Trump tries to turn it into a stage so he can own it.

Whether he succeeds procedurally is only part of the question.

The deeper question is whether the public will continue to defend the boring distance that keeps the law from becoming a club.

Because once justice is aimed as a weapon, it rarely returns to being blind.

Trump's effort to aim the DOJ also creates a second, quieter consequence: it changes how ordinary people talk about law. In the sequel, people begin to speak about indictments the way they speak about sports scores. "We got one." "They got away with it." "The refs are rigged." The language of justice becomes the language of factional entertainment.

That shift is catastrophic because it teaches the public to celebrate punishment without understanding standards. It teaches people to confuse accusations with proof. It teaches supporters to demand prosecutions when emotionally satisfying and to dismiss prosecutions when inconvenient. Justice becomes a switch you flip depending on whose name is on the headline.

Once that switch is normalized, it does not stay contained to Trump. Future leaders inherit a public trained to expect vengeance. Every administration becomes vulnerable to the same demand: punish the other side or be accused of weakness. The DOJ becomes a hostage to public appetite.

This is how democratic erosion often works. It is not only leaders who change institutions; it is audiences who change what they will tolerate. Trump's attempts to weaponize the DOJ are an education program in cynicism. They teach citizens that the law is not a shared shield but a private sword.

And a sword, once drawn as a political tool, rarely returns fully to its sheath.

One final consequence is the chilling of legitimacy itself. When Trump frames lawful limits as "witch hunts," he does not merely protect himself—he attacks the concept of neutral adjudication. That attack makes it harder for any future prosecution, even a justified one, to be trusted by the public. The institution becomes less capable not because it loses authority on paper, but because it loses authority in the imagination.

And when authority collapses in the imagination, the rule of law becomes a rumor.

CHAPTER 25: THE FRIEND YOU NEVER KNEW

There are moments when denial stops being defensive and becomes Jeffrey Epstein, who enters this book carefully, because the topic demands it.

Not because the story is obscure, but because it is radioactive: it attracts speculation, invites exaggeration, and tempts people into turning a real pattern of exploitation into a political prop. That temptation is itself a symptom of the era—everything becomes content, even the ugliest harm.

This chapter does not attempt to litigate guilt by proximity.

It examines something narrower and, in its own way, more revealing: Donald Trump's relationship with truth when confronted with uncomfortable associations, and how denial functions as a governing reflex rather than a momentary defense.

Epstein is publicly known as a wealthy financier who was accused and convicted in one case of sex offenses, and who faced additional serious allegations of sexual exploitation before his death. His network included prominent people. His social world intersected with elite circles across politics, finance, and entertainment.

That intersection is not, by itself, proof of wrongdoing by everyone within it.

But it is evidence of proximity.

And proximity, when publicly documented, creates a challenge for anyone whose brand depends on moral dominance: you must explain what the proximity means, how deep it was, and what you knew or did not know. You must answer the simplest question of all:

Were you close, or were you not?

In Trump's case, the public record includes years in which Epstein moved within social circles connected to Trump's world. There are photographs and accounts of shared appearances in public settings; there are reports of acquaintance-level familiarity that Trump at times acknowledges and at other times minimizes.

Trump's approach to this discomfort is consistent with his broader pattern:

He does not clarify.

He contests.

He rebrands.

When the association looks harmless, it becomes casual: "I knew him," "everyone knew him," "he was around." When the association becomes morally dangerous, it becomes distant: "not close," "barely knew," "not really," "I cut him off."

This is not unique to this topic.

It is Trump's rhetorical survival system: adjust the story to match the danger level, not the evidence level.

The question, then, is not whether Trump is responsible for Epstein's crimes.

The question is whether Trump's public responses reflect a stable relationship with truth or a flexible one.

A stable relationship with truth is boring:

Yes, we knew each other.

Here is the nature of the relationship.

Here is what I knew at the time.

Here is what I did when I learned more.

Here is the record, and here is my accountability.

Trump does not prefer boring.

Trump prefers dominance.

So, the responses often sound less like an explanation and more like management. The goal is not to inform the public. The goal is to reduce liability—social, political, reputational—by narrowing the frame until the association looks trivial.

Denial becomes a tool for shrinking reality.

And shrinking reality is the theme of this book.

From crowd sizes to hurricane maps to election claims, Trump repeatedly treats facts as negotiable if negotiating them protects the brand. The mechanism is always the same: do not concede. Do not clarify if clarification admits vulnerability. Attack the framing. Question the motive. Replace the question with a more flattering one.

Instead of "How close were you?" the story becomes "Why are they trying to smear me?"

That pivot is powerful because it changes the posture from accountability to persecution. It is the same pivot used in courtrooms, investigations, and scandals.

The leader is not being questioned.

He is being hunted.

Once that frame is established, evidence becomes optional. Critics become enemies. Journalists become conspirators. The public is invited to choose loyalty over scrutiny.

This does not resolve the association.

It dissolves it into tribal conflict.

And tribal conflict is where Trump is most comfortable because tribal conflict has no referee. It requires no proof. It rewards confidence. It punishes doubt. It allows a leader to survive without clarifying anything, as long as the base remains emotionally aligned.

The Epstein association is difficult because it is not a policy debate. It is a moral reflection. It forces a leader to address the boundaries of his world, the company he kept, the judgment he exercised, and the honesty he brings to public trust.

Trump responds by making the mirror foggy.

He emphasizes distance. He shifts timelines. He highlights moments that suggest disassociation. He minimizes familiarity. He uses absolute language when useful and vague language when pressed.

The public is left with a haze.

That haze functions as defense. If the story is unclear, accountability is harder. If the record is muddy, outrage loses focus. If details are contested endlessly, fatigue arrives.

Fatigue is Trump's ally.

Fatigue is how scandals become background noise. It is how the public shrugs at contradictions it would once have treated as disqualifying. It is how a culture normalizes denial as a style of leadership rather than a symptom of it.

This chapter also matters because it illustrates the moral cost of a flexible relationship with truth.

When a leader habitually treats truth as negotiable, the public becomes trained to treat truth as partisan. Even serious allegations of exploitation become filtered through political loyalty. People stop asking, "What is true?" and start asking, "Who is using this?"

That shift is dangerous because it degrades the capacity of society to confront harm.

Epstein's story is fundamentally about exploitation of underage girls and abuse of power. The victims deserve seriousness. They deserve a public that can recognize wrongdoing without turning it into a partisan weapon. They deserve institutions capable of accountability.

When the conversation becomes tribal, the victims disappear.

Trump's denial patterns contribute to this disappearance by redirecting attention away from clarity and toward conflict. If the story is framed as a smear campaign, the moral center is replaced with grievance. The focus shifts from harm to reputation.

Reputation becomes the issue.

Harm becomes background.

This is the inversion the book repeatedly exposes.

The chapter does not need to prove what Trump did or did not do to make its point. It needs only to show how Trump handles questions that threaten his self-image.

He minimizes.

He redirects.

He contests.

He reframes.

He attacks the asker.

He insists on his own narrative as the only legitimate one.

This is "truth" as a tool rather than truth as obligation.

And because Trump is president, that posture matters beyond biography. A leader who cannot tell the truth about the uncomfortable parts of his own associations is unlikely to tell the truth about uncomfortable parts of governance.

The habit does not compartmentalize.

It spreads.

The Epstein chapter is placed last in this volume not to end with scandal, but to end with a theme: denial is not an isolated tactic. It is the operating system. It is how power protects itself from shame, from

113

consequence, and from the simple discipline of saying, "Here are the facts."

This book is titled Grabbing America by the P because it is about coercion—coercion of bodies, of institutions, of truth. Epstein's story is a grotesque example of how power can exploit vulnerability. Trump's association with Epstein, and his shifting public posture about that association, becomes a final mirror of a larger pattern: when confronted with moral discomfort, Trump tries to bend reality rather than confront it.

The mirror is not comfortable.

But it is consistent.

And because Trump remains in office for years to come, this ending is not closure. It is a warning that the pattern persists.

The chapter closes with a simple refusal to let fog be the final word:

Truth is not a vibe.

Truth is not a brand.

Truth is not a loyalty test.

Truth is the minimum cost of living in a democracy.

When a leader treats it as optional, the country eventually pays the bill.

This is why the placement of this chapter matters. Ending here is not an attempt to sensationalize. It is an attempt to show the endpoint of a governing style built on denial. When a leader is practiced at bending facts, even morally grave questions become merely another PR puzzle: reduce exposure, reframe the ask, shift attention, deny the premise, accuse the critic.

That is not leadership.

It is brand defense.

And brand defense, when practiced long enough, produces a citizenry that doubts everything except allegiance. In that environment, legitimate calls for accountability become harder to hear, because people assume every demand for truth is really a demand for advantage.

The victims of exploitation deserve better than that environment. They deserve a public capable of moral seriousness. They deserve institutions that can investigate without being screamed at. They deserve leaders who can say, without theatrical spin, "The harm happened, and we will face it honestly."

This chapter is therefore less about Epstein's infamous network than about what that network reveals: how power moves through elite circles, how reputations are managed, and how denial can become a reflex that protects status at the expense of clarity.

If the Trumpology series continues—as it must—this theme will return. Not because this specific association is the center of everything, but because the reflex is. The refusal to speak plainly, the instinct to fog the mirror, the habit of treating truth as optional—those are the engines that keep the sequel running.

And engines that run on denial do not stop. They only move on to the next road.

POSTSCRIPT: THIS IS NOT THE END

This book ends because it must.

Not because the story is finished.

Donald Trump remains president. Power remains concentrated. Patterns remain intact. The methods documented in these pages continue to operate, evolve, and adapt in real time. What you have read is not a retrospective. It is a snapshot taken mid-motion.

History has not closed the file.

If this book feels unresolved, that is not a failure of authorship. It is an honest reflection of the moment we are living in. The forces described here do not pause for publication schedules. They do not wait for analysis to catch up. They move forward, reshaping institutions, language, and expectations while the country argues about whether the reshaping is happening at all.

This is the danger of living inside the story.

When power is ongoing, clarity arrives slowly. Patterns become visible only after repetition. Damage is often understood only after normalization. By the time consequences feel obvious, they are already embedded.

That is why this book exists.

Grabbing America by the P does not attempt to predict the future. It documents a method. And methods, once identified, tend to persist. They adapt to resistance. They learn from failure. They refine themselves.

The sequel is still being written.

There will be more policies framed as a necessity. More institutions are pressured into loyalty. More crises announced loudly and resolved quietly—if at all. More declarations that precede verification. More efforts to bend law, history, and memory without openly breaking them.

There will also be more resistance.

History does not move in one direction. Institutions do not fail all at once. Truth does not disappear overnight. The struggle between accountability and dominance is ongoing, uneven, and unresolved.

That struggle is the subject of the books to come.

The Trumpology series exists because this era cannot be understood in a single volume. Each phase introduces new adaptations. Each reaction produces new strategies. Each exposure teaches power how to hide better next time.

Future volumes will track what happens next:

How institutions respond under sustained pressure.

How public fatigue reshapes accountability.

How truth survives—or doesn't—inside a permanent performance.

How democracy absorbs stress without collapsing, and where it cracks.

This book is the opening record, not the final verdict.

If you are unsettled by this ending, stay with that discomfort. It is the appropriate response to an unfinished story. It is also the reason to keep reading, questioning, and documenting what comes next.

Because the most dangerous chapters of any political era are the ones written after people stop paying attention.

The next book in the Trumpology series will pick up where this one cannot—tracking what unfolds when repetition hardens into doctrine and consequence becomes legacy.

This is not the end.

It is the warning before the next chapter.